Teaching by Topics

Teaching by Topics

Peter Rance

Headmaster, Hertingfordbury Primary School

Ward Lock Educational

10565

7062 3030 2 Hardback
7062 3292 5 Paperback
First published 1968
Reprinted 1969

Designed by Robin Kempster
Set in Monotype Times New Roman 11 on 12 point
Made in England by
Redwood Press Limited
Trowbridge & London

Contents

Acknowledgments

My grateful thanks are due to my teaching colleagues for their help; to the children of Hertingfordbury School who appear in the photographs reproduced by kind permission of Scholastic Souvenir Co Ltd, Blackpool; and to Miss Ann Parker, Schools Librarian, Hertford for her co-operation and encouragement.

Introduction

The aim of this book is to show how 'topic' work can be developed and organized throughout a primary school so that the children can proceed by graduated steps towards the stage where they can undertake a study of a subject on their own, without the guidance of a teacher.

In recent years 'topic' work has aroused the interest of a great many teachers, but few books have been written by practising teachers on the subject. Perhaps the reason for this is the fact that teaching being a form of dedicated hard labour and so greatly demanding in the amount of mental and physical energy expended, has left little time to spare for the preparation and writing of such a work. If this is so, you may well ask why I undertook the task of writing this book. To be explicit it was for two reasons.

Firstly, I believe that since the Education Act of 1870 the major advances in education have been made primarily in the field of governmental organization and administration.

Secondly, I believe that since the Education Act of 1944 we have witnessed the early stages of a revolution in our methods of teaching. The books, apparatus, machines and ideas now coming into practical service in our schools will bring a new dimension to educational exploration.

This spirit of progress is best reflected in our present attitude to the teaching of reading and mathematics in the primary school. Here the child's needs are increasingly taking precedence over the academic demands of the subject matter, particularly when opportunities arise for encouraging a child to discover knowledge for himself.

To assist the reader in finding his way this book has been divided into three parts. The first is an explanation of the foundations and terminology of topics, the second a detailed scheme of work for grading topics and the final part which offers some solutions to the everyday problems of teaching topics in the classroom. The book is also designed as a work of reference to be consulted in the classroom as practical problems arise in the course of a topic.

Part One | Chapter One

The Origin of Topics

Topics, projects, centres of interest and environmental studies have long been regarded as effective and attractive teaching methods, but teachers tied to a strict syllabus of work sometimes find that such techniques cannot be relied upon to hammer home those specific items of knowledge demanded by many public examinations. As a result, doubts have arisen as to their ultimate usefulness, and some teachers feel that children can acquire such knowledge faster by the older methods of teaching. To a limited extent these opinions can be justified, but only if a child is regarded as a tankard to be crammed with its full pint of knowledge from the teacher's inexhaustible jug. Obviously this should not be taken to mean that topic work absolves a teacher from her or his obligation to see that the children are given a firm grounding in the basic principles of reading, writing and mathematics for this must always be the first task.

With the development of new attitudes to teaching, however, it is quite clear that more and more emphasis is being placed on how a child is learning and less on the quantity of what is being learnt. In fact, the main aim of these methods is to see that the child acquires a greater ability to control his own methods of collecting, collating and storing knowledge.

When teachers seek information about these child-centred methods they quickly discover a problem of terminology, for there appears to be no universally agreed definition of the words *topic*, *project*, *centres of interest* and *environmental studies*, as used in their educational sense. Thus we have a situation that, while they are used in all kinds of educational establishments to cover many aspects of similar ideas, it is very difficult to grasp their precise meaning. In these circumstances there is little point in discussing topics until we have stated in very clear terms how these words should be employed, taking into account the varying extant opinions. Indeed, as it is their great similarity that has caused this language barrier, we can best tackle the problem by first listing their similarities:

1 They all make a definite attempt to break away from the conventional methods of teaching in a way that places more importance on the child than on the subject under study.
2 They try to allow a child to construct its own methods of approach to knowledge, and in the long run to form its own opinions about it.
3 They all give the child an opportunity to 'learn how to learn'.
4 They usually succeed in breaking down the artificial barriers that have been erected around the various academic subjects in the past, although in recent years it has become quite common practice for one subject to have a major influence on the way the completed topic is presented.
5 They all seek to make the child's interest in the real world the platform from which a natural, as opposed to an artificial, method of acquiring knowledge is evolved.

While these methods have much in common, however, it is also true to say that there are certain subtle differences and, by considering each one in turn, I should like to suggest how their individual characteristics can be recognized.

Projects

At the beginning of the twentieth century, an American educationist, W. H. Kilpatrick, a colleague of John Dewey, suggested that a method of teaching could be evolved by putting the emphasis on autonomous learning by the pupil. The American word for a student's model in woodwork or metalwork at this time was 'project', and the word carried with it the implication that the article was made from materials obtained in their raw state. This implication still exists in our present use of the word 'project' which invites pupils to pursue an investigation into a subject from the basic facts available, irrespective of any boundaries which might be thought to exist between the more conventional academic subjects.

If this is so, how would a group of children carry out a project; for example, to establish which washing powder washes clothes cleanest?

Clearly, the project will require the use of various types of washing powder, and include practical experiments in washing, drying and ironing clothes. Mathematics will be used to collate and assess the statistics. Chemistry will be required for analysing the contents of each type of soap powder. Art may be used to display the findings of the experiment or to assess the quality of the advertisements used by the soap manufacturers. A study of the standard of English used in advertisement copy can be made, and the children encouraged to write and set to music advertising jingles of their own.

Even from this short outline it can be seen that projects tend to combine a number of conventional subjects such as mathematics, science, art and music so that children can obtain a better understanding of the subject under investigation.

How then do projects differ from other child-centred methods of teaching we have mentioned?

Characteristics of projects

1 No limits are set to the eventual scope of the subject being studied.
2 There is always an element of research in a project. This research usually arises from a desire to inquire more deeply into facts which have been observed or acquired previously.
3 Many or all the conventional subjects may be put to use in order that the subject matter can be adequately studied.

Centres of interest

About fifty years ago a pioneer of education in Belgium, Dr Ovide Decroly, first used the phrase 'centre of interest'. Decroly's aim was to break away from the dull and sterile teaching found in the primary schools of his time and enliven the children's work by undertaking the study of subjects which were of basic human interest to them—food, housing, clothing, animals, plants and so on. His object was to harness the children's interest in a subject by getting them to see, to think, to act and to express themselves about it in ways that would lead to an improvement in their reading, writing and arithmetic.

Jean Lee Hunt, the translator of Decroly's work, described his methods as the 'Belgian Project Method' but, talking of them himself, Decroly said, 'We must organize the environment to afford adequate stimuli for tendencies favourable to development.'

Unfortunately many teachers, when describing their own work in this field, put an interpretation on the phrase 'centre of interest' which is far removed from that employed in the book, *The Decroly Class*, written by Amelie Hamaide. With such an excellent book available to speak for itself, it is enough for our purpose that the main characteristics of this type of approach are listed for us in Chapter XI of the book.

Characteristics of centres of interest

1 The subject matter is nearly always drawn from nature.
2 The stages of development in a subject are planned in advance by the teacher. Some centres of interest are planned to last at least one year.
3 The work is graded in its development throughout the school. Added to this, a system for repeating the techniques learnt must be devised.

Environmental studies

The ideas of both Dewey and Decroly percolated through the educational systems of many countries and resulted in various attempts to make 'child-centred omelettes' from the eggs laid by the conventional subjects like geography, history and nature study. The environment was studied in ever-widening concentric circles by children who used their knowledge of other subjects to get a better understanding, first of their immediate surrounding, then of their country and later of the rest of the world.

These developments, from the early part of the nineteen-twenties onwards, are now commonly known as environmental studies. The great similarity between all the above mentioned systems of teaching has already been noted, and environmental studies can best be described as a cross between 'projects' and 'centres of interest'.

Characteristics of environmental studies

1 The introductory stage of the work is limited to subjects inspired by the local environment. Unlike centres of interest, these subjects need not be taken from nature. Environmental studies can include, for example, the study of a local industry, a local church, a geographical feature of the local countryside or any other similar subject.
2 Environmental studies always presuppose that a certain amount of work will be undertaken outside the classroom.
3 The accepted implication with this work is that, although initially the subject matter is inspired by something in the local environment, the final studies will lead much further afield.

Topics

In recent years, a better understanding of the teaching problems involved in projects, centres of interest and environmental studies has led to many teachers evolving a more limited technique of child-centred learning which now comes under the title of 'topics'. The word seems to have no historical background when used in its educational sense and for the purpose of this book it can be defined as follows.

Topic work is a child-centred activity where structure and organization can be progressively developed throughout a school. It requires the content of the normal curricular subjects to be used so that the pupil can develop a simple but logical method of systematically seeking, absorbing, organizing and recording knowledge. This process should be allowed to flourish in a situation which enables the child to make a free choice, within predetermined limits, of the subject he wishes to study and encourages him to create an end product commensurate with his mental and physical abilities. The end product of such a course of study may be the result of a combined effort on the part of a group of children, or the individual studies of one child.*

*By 'normal curricular subjects' are meant those subjects which are generally found in the primary school curriculum such as history, English, geography, mathematics, art, etc.

The remainder of this book elaborates and exemplifies this definition, but a summary of the topic's characteristics is given here.

Characteristics of topics

1 A child is free to study any subject within the limits approved of by the teacher.

2 Topics are designed, in most cases, to take advantage of the abundance of general knowledge so easily available via all the modern means of communication—newspapers, periodicals, books, films, radio and television and manufacturers' brochures.

3 In the younger classes of the junior school, class topics require a carefully planned and prepared introduction to the subject matter.

4 The teaching time required to complete projects, centres of interest and environmental studies is usually measured in weeks, whereas topics can normally be completed in hours.

5 Topics can be graded so that their internal organization can be improved and developed one stage at a time. This helps the child gradually to improve its own techniques for acquiring fresh knowledge.

While topic work is usually referred to as a method of teaching it is better described as a method of 'learning how to learn'.

Thus as children set out to obtain knowledge of a subject via topic work it is the teacher's main task to create actively the situation and atmosphere which is most conducive to this learning process.

Obviously, some direct instruction in this method of learning must be given from time to time so that the children understand what is required of them, hence the term 'graded' topics, i.e., graded to teach techniques of learning.

Part One | Chapter Two

Topic Terminology

When a new appreciation of a subject is undertaken, it often creates the need for a better definition of terms already in common use. This is certainly the case with topic work. In fact, many of the words and phrases at present connected with topic work are so loosely defined as to be almost useless for a detailed study of the subject.

The establishment of a short working terminology for topics must therefore be one of our first tasks. It is also essential at an early stage to differentiate clearly between the two possible types of topic and the various methods of organization which can be used to carry out these topics. All topics will of course conform with the definition they have been given in the previous chapter.

Two Types of topic

The graded topic

This is the name given to topics in which the teacher deliberately sets out to teach children new methods for obtaining, selecting, recording and presenting knowledge. In graded topics the *method* of carrying out the topic is of major importance, the subject matter a secondary consideration.

For example, a graded topic could have the following aim:
to carry out a graded/class topic based on a subject with which the children are unfamiliar. The topic must teach the children how to discover, select and rewrite, mainly from the textbooks available, the information they require and also show them how to organize and present such information in a booklet or folder.

During such a topic, the children will obviously acquire a greater understanding of the subject matter being studied, but this is not of prime importance. As far as the teacher is concerned, success or failure in a graded topic will depend upon whether the new techniques of topic work, which it was intended to teach, were learnt or not. Thus graded topics are primarily concerned with two things; first teaching children how to improve their ability to acquire knowledge and, secondly, to develop new forms of topic organization.

Obviously these techniques need to be practised and exploited in subsequent topics where the main aim is to obtain greater knowledge of the subject matter being studied. This type of topic, where the subject matter is of first importance, is called the *subject topic*.

The subject topic

The major aim of the subject topic is to encourage children to acquire a wide range of knowledge concerning a particular subject. For example, a subject topic could have the following aim: to teach the children as many details as possible about the life of Captain Cook.

We can see that in this type of topic the *subject matter* is of first importance and that the exploitation of techniques of organization taught during the preceding graded topics is incidental. However, the organization of a subject topic is, of course, always based upon the careful training the children have previously received. Once all graded topics have been mastered, the question of how each subject topic shall be organized is solely a matter of choosing the method most suited to the subject being studied.

Methods of organizing a topic

In this section, the various words and phrases used to describe different kinds of topic organization are defined.

An individual topic

A complete topic carried out by one child.

A group topic

A topic undertaken by a group of children on a subject unconnected with the work being carried out by the rest of the class. There are usually between four and six children in a group.

A class topic

A topic carried out by all the children in a class contributing to a central theme, either in groups or individually.

A varying number of combinations can be developed from these three basic kinds of organization, but for all practical purposes only two need to be defined. Both of these concern the relationship of groups within a Class Topic.

Group organization within a class topic

An independent group

In some class topics, each group is a self-sufficient unit which only contributes one independent section to the central theme of the topic. Such groups are called independent groups.

For example, a class topic on the subject 'A bar of fruit and nut chocolate' could have independent groups working on: cocoa/milk/sugar cane/sugar beet/dried fruits/citrus fruits/paper.

Thus, while each group will be seeking information about the central theme, its researches are unlikely to affect, or impinge on, those of other groups.

A linked group

On the other hand, when a group collaborates with its neighbours, and useful information is circulated between them as each works on its own aspect of the main theme of a class topic, they are called linked groups.

For example, a class topic on 'The Normans' could include linked groups working on: William I/castles/saxon villages/hunting/law and order/pilgrimages/Hereward the Wake/Domesday Book/churches.

In this case, the researches carried out by one group will overlap those of the other groups and, on occasions, even require their active cooperation.

Development of a topic
Critical path shown by bold line

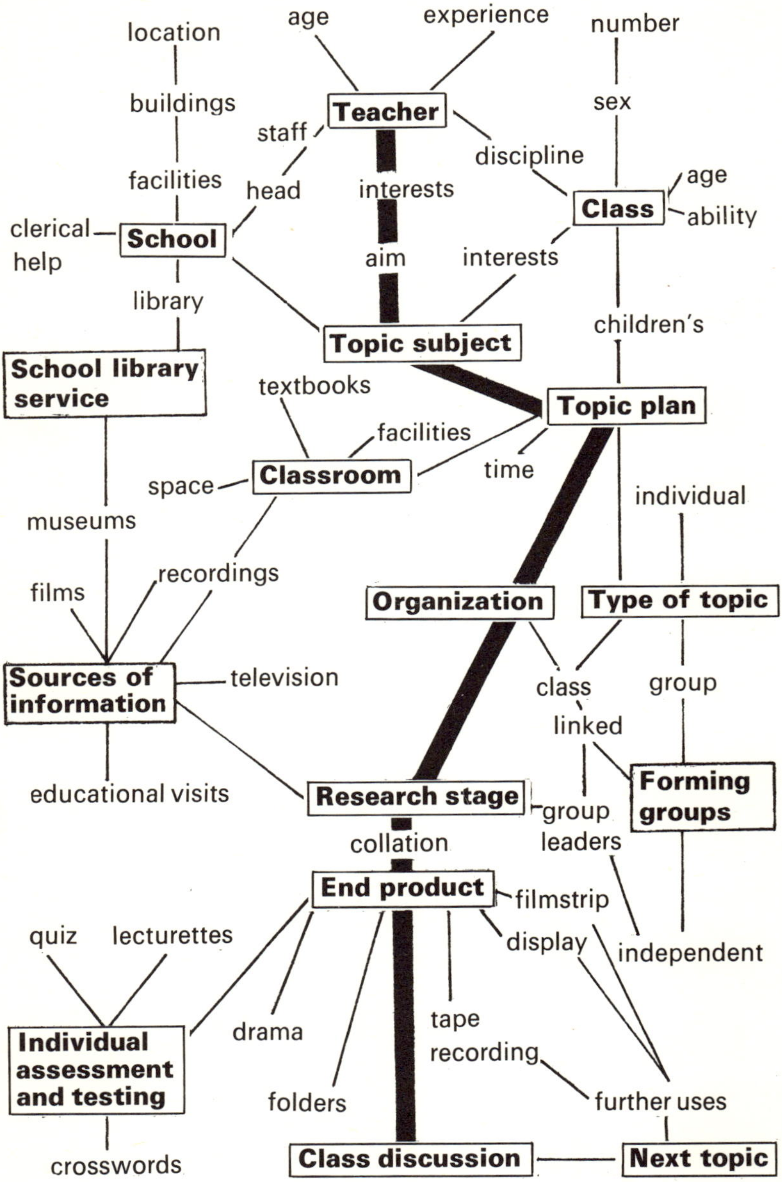

Part One | Chapter Three

The Basic Organization of Topics

The background of English

While this book is almost exclusively concerned with the organization of topic work throughout the primary school, it would not be correct to discuss this subject without first referring to its influence on the children's use of the English language.

From the very earliest stages of topic work the opportunities for all kinds of creative English are considerable, and, just as the children become increasingly competent at assimilating factual knowledge, so their mastery of their native tongue expands as well.

Although English will percolate into every fibre of this work there is also a place for the topic which deliberately sets out to teach all aspects of the language. An example of this type of creative English topic is described in Chapter Nine.

The basic outline

Having stressed the ever-present relationship between language and topics, let us turn to the question of their organization. Many teachers use projects and topics in their classroom, but most are still very receptive to suggestions which will improve their work. In addition to this there are teachers who are relatively inexperienced in this type of work. How should such a teacher embark upon a topic?

Ideally she should be able to seek advice from her more experienced colleagues and be able to base her ideas upon the techniques of topic work her class has already learnt lower down the school. Unfortunately not all schools have a scheme of work for grading their topics in such a way that the simpler forms of topic organization are first taught to the younger children, so that they learn progressively the more complex techniques.

A complete scheme for grading topics is given in Part Two Chapter Four.

Such a scheme of graded topics takes time to establish itself in a junior school. Where it is not practised, any teacher new to this work will be well advised to carry out a few simple topics first. By doing so, both she and the children will have a chance to familiarize themselves with this method of working. Once topic work has been started however, good teachers will quickly discover that all topics have a similar basic plan.

A closer examination of this plan will show that it consists of five loosely linked stages:

1 The teacher's preparation of the subject.
2 The introduction of the subject to the class.
3 The organization of the subject with the class.
4 The children's research into the subject matter.
5 The end product.

Once these five stages have been carried out, it is also quite usual to have a discussion session during which the topic is reviewed, and suggestions made for the improvement of subsequent topics.

Bearing the five stages in mind, how should a teacher, with very little experience of this work, embark on a topic when faced with a class of 40 ten-year-old children who have never undertaken a topic before?

To answer this question let us follow a teacher through a simple topic and see how each stage prepares the way for those that follow.

Stage 1 Teacher preparation

The teacher's preparation stage begins immediately she decides to do a topic, for she must decide the central theme for the topic, the limits within which she intends the children to work and the kind of end product she requires.

If she has had very little previous experience with topics, the teacher will be wise to confine herself to the simplest of topic themes such as a period in history, the life cycle of a plant or animal or the production process of an industry. Some examples of these have been provided at the end of this chapter.

All these subjects have a very obvious sequence of development upon which the children can build their topic. They also have the added advantage that there is usually plenty of background information readily available within the school's existing stock of library and textbooks. In most schools and homes it will be found that history is the subject about which most general knowledge is easily obtainable and therefore a period in history is, perhaps, the easiest topic to undertake.

Let us suppose that a perusal of her school's history syllabus reveals that the teacher is responsible for introducing her class to some of the famous people who lived between 1688 and 1800. Let us also suppose that:

a The time allotted to this task is one term.
b The teacher realizes that she will need a fairly long time to prepare for the topic.
c She decides to use the topic mainly as a means of correlating, and adding to, the knowledge she has imparted during the first part of the term.

The teacher could well give her topic the title 'The Eighteenth Century', which will immediately fix the historical time limits of the subject matter, and yet leave the children free to include a wide range of information on subjects other than the famous people they will have already studied.

Having chosen a title for the central theme of the topic the teacher must acquaint herself through books, filmstrips and previous topics (if any) with the scope of the subject to see if it is broad enough, and interesting enough for her class. She must assess carefully the amount of information available to the children within their classroom, their school and their immediate locality. If such information is found to be lacking the teacher must either choose a more congenial central theme, or spend time in collecting information sources before the topic starts. For a list of possible information sources see page 119. Generally it will be found that in most counties of Britain the School Library Service is the best source of useful books for teachers preparing a topic.

Once she has firmly decided on the central theme of the topic and assessed its potential scope, the teacher will have possessed herself of enough knowledge of the various facets of the subject to enable her to prepare a tentative outline plan for each group assignment. With most historical topics the chronological order of events provides the simplest outline plan, since it makes the assignment of each group's subject matter depend upon a fixed number of years.

As this is a class of 40 children and the theme is the eighteenth century, the outline plan might well consist of periods of twenty years so that the class is split into five groups with eight children each. For example this can be laid out as follows:

Topic on the eighteenth century

Group 1	Group 2	Group 3	Group 4	Group 5
1700 to 1720	1720 to 1740	1740 to 1760	1760 to 1780	1780 to 1800

If this simple outline plan is written on the blackboard at an early stage of the topic it will help the children to see how the work is to be organized later on.

Stage 2 The introduction of the subject

Now the scene is set in the teacher's mind and it is up to her to arouse the children's interest in the chosen theme. In the youngest junior classes this may need careful planning, but as the children grow older quite ordinary suggestions can start them off on a full-blooded quest for additional knowledge about a subject which takes their interest.

How to organize a stimulating introduction to a topic for young children is not always easy, but the problem appears to have six basic solutions:

a An educational visit to a place of interest to children. This out-of-school activity can be something as simple as a half-hour nature walk, or as complicated as a day trip to a nearby city.
b A special programme on television, or radio. A film or film-strip can often inspire the start of a topic.
c A well prepared story, picture display, or lesson can sometimes generate interest and call for more detailed study.
d A visit from someone outside school life, such as a policeman, fireman, farmer, shopkeeper, traffic warden or nurse to talk about their work, usually starts a flow of questions from the children, which can be answered by a topic.
e When the children become experienced in carrying out a topic the teacher can simply announce that the class is going to undertake a study of a particular theme. As the children enjoy topic work there are normally no problems.
f By introducing and undertaking a new activity or experience for the children.

As the children carrying out this eighteenth-century topic are ten-year-olds it is quite possible that the idea of making a large book will be novel enough to appeal to them. It is likely to excite their interest even more if they are told they can display the book for other classes to read once it is finished. This will apply especially in schools where topic work has not been carried out before.

Because the teacher has sensibly based her first topic upon a period in history with which the children are already familiar, they will be able to participate in an initial discussion of the subject with her, without the need to refer to books first. Similarly she will, because of her own preplanning, be able to suggest during the discussion, facets of the subject which the children may find it easy and interesting to investigate. Thus by discussion and mutual consent between teacher and class, a list of suitable assignments for further study can be constructed on the blackboard in very rough outline. This will probably be similar to the outline the teacher made at the preparation stage.

Next follows a period of between two and three hours when the class should be allowed to discover for themselves the various sources of information available, the scope of the subject, and to form individual preferences for one particular assignment connected with the topic's main theme.

All these activities are, of course, building up to the following stage when the general organization of both the class and the subject takes place.

Stage 3 Organization of the subject with the class

Having, as it were, allowed the class to taste the topic on their own the teacher should help the children organize themselves into groups so that children with similar interests can work together. While doing this, remember that a well prepared topic always ensures that a balanced investigation of a subject takes place and that the end product adequately covers most aspects of the central theme.

Before grouping actually takes place, the class should revise and consolidate the outline plan of possible assignments written on the blackboard. This could well result in the suggestion of a large number of further subjects which are worthy of investigation. If the list becomes too large to be adequately displayed on the blackboard, it must be duplicated.

A duplicated outline plan for the eighteenth-century topic might well appear as follows:

THE EIGHTEENTH CENTURY—*Topic group assignments*

Group 1 1700–1720

1701 James II dies in Italy/1702 William III dies, Act of Settlement, Anne crowned/1702–13 War of Spanish Succession, Duke of Marlborough, Blenheim, Ramillies/1703 Samuel Pepys dies/1712 Newcomen invents his steam engine/1713 Treaty of Utrecht/1714 George I crowned/1715 James Edward Stuart invades England/1718 William Penn, founder of Pennsylvania, dies/1720 The South Sea Bubble/Changes in design of dress, furniture, housing during the reign of Queen Anne.

Group 2 1720–1740

1721 Walpole Prime Minister/Writings of Swift, Defoe and Pope/1723 Sir Christopher Wren born/1725 Clive of India born/1727 George I dies, James Wolfe born/1732 George

Washington born/1733 Kay's Flying Shuttle invented/1736 James Watt born/1739 War of Jenkin's Ear, John Wesley founds Methodism, Dick Turpin hanged at York/Developments in Industry and Farming/Details of military uniforms and equipment.

Group 3 1740–1760

1743–8 War of Austrian Succession/1743 George II at Battle of Dettingen/1745 Bonnie Prince Charlie invades England/1746 Culloden/1751 Clive at the Siege of Arcot/1752 Gregorian Calendar introduced in England/1756–63 The Seven Years' War/1756 The Black Hole of Calcutta/1757 Clive at Plassey, Admiral Byng shot/1758 First canal built for the Duke of Bridgewater/1759 Wolfe at Quebec, William Wilberforce born/Dr Johnson's new Dictionary, Handel composing music.

Group 4 1760–1780

1760 George II dies, George III crowned/1764 Hargreaves invents Spinning Jenny/1765–85 Enclosure of Common land at its highest level/1768–79 Captain Cook's voyages to the South Seas/1769 Mark Isambard Brunel born/1773 The Boston Tea Party/1774–83 The American War of Independence/1774–9 Crompton's Mule invented/1776 James Watt improves the steam engine/Life of Benjamin Franklin/Paintings of Reynolds and Gainsborough.

Group 5 1780–1800

1780 Elizabeth Fry born/1783 Treaty of Versailles/1781 George Stephenson born/1785 *The Times* newspaper founded, Royal Mail Coaches started/1787 Cartwright invents Power Loom/1788 Trial of Warren Hastings/1789 French Revolution begins/1798 Nelson at Battle of the Nile/Life of Napoleon Bonaparte/Poetry of Burns, Wordsworth, Coleridge/Details of improvements in road making and coach building.

With this final outline established the teacher can now help the children organize themselves into assignment groups so that their individual preferences are catered for. Any teacher in difficulties with this process should refer to page 132 for help.

At the end of this organizational stage each child should be ready to undertake a study of a subject in which it is interested. Each child should also be a member of a group of children interested in other subjects connected with the same historical period. For example a child interested in Bonnie Prince Charlie should find himself working in Group 3 (1740 to 1760) and a child interested in Elizabeth Fry with Group 5 (1780 to 1800). Obviously a group of eight children cannot produce a comprehensive account on all the subjects listed on the duplicated sheet for their assignment, but it would be quite reasonable to expect at least four detailed accounts. Some of the other dates, people, events etc., could quite possibly be covered by short précis of one hundred words, or only mentioned within one of the longer accounts.

Normally it should be possible to complete this stage of organization in about two hours or less.

Stage 4 Children's research

The title of this stage speaks for itself, and may take many hours to complete depending on the availability of information and the amount of interest the topic arouses among the children. Many unproductive avenues of investigation will be pursued as well as successful ones, but it has been found that even these apparently unsuccessful researches lead to a rapid widening of the children's store of general knowledge. Also they frequently act as starting points for individual topics later on.

The role of the teacher throughout this stage is to help the children discover the information they require, oversee the organization of each group's work to see that each child has a suitable amount of work for its capabilities and to encourage everyone to adopt a personal approach to presenting the information obtained. If this last point is not emphasized the children tend to copy large extracts from books. How to prevent this is discussed on page 64.

During all these activities the teacher should not attempt to impose her own answers to the problems that arise, and only as a last resort should she suggest possible solutions. The children must always be encouraged to find things out for themselves, since they will often learn faster by making their own mistakes. As the work proceeds the teacher who keeps a friendly eye on each group will easily recognize the moment when it is ready to correlate the results of its labours. In a historical topic of this nature the only pattern to emerge from this correlating process will be chronological. With some topics however, the process of correlating a group's work will reveal glaring ommissions or facets which can lead to further new work for the class as a whole. This is unlikely to happen with the topic under consideration as the historical assignment allocated to each group is so wide that the children will only be able to present a brief outline of the more interesting aspects of the period for which they are responsible.

Once each group has successfully arranged its findings in an attractive sequence, all the groups should combine to produce an end product which displays their work in a logical manner. In this case it will be a large book.

Again this activity can reveal ommissions such as the lack of a complete index for the book, and the need for a well designed front cover and numbers for each page. All these tasks will have to be completed quickly if the final product is to be finished before the children's interest wanes.

Stage 5 The end product

This topic started with the intention of producing, as an end product, a book which the class could show to the rest of the school. The size, shape, binding, covering, and chapter headings should have been agreed at the Introduction stage so that everyone was quite clear from the start how large any drawings, newspaper cuttings, photographs and pages of written work had to be.

Once completed, the final book should be made available for study by the class itself for a while and a revision lesson taken on its contents. Such lessons can be taken by means of a duplicated questionnaire like the one shown on page 164. Alternatively an inter-group quiz on the topic's contents can be held verbally. Alongside this revision process should go at least one short discussion period designed to assess the qualities of the end product, and thereby encourage the children to suggest various ways of improving the standard of their work.

After reading this book it is hoped that teachers will be able to lead this assessment discussion by contributing new ideas as each new grade is reached.

Conclusion

The intention of this chapter on the basic elements of a topic is to tempt teachers to experiment with topics of their own before starting the series of graded topics suggested in Part Two of this book. To make their task easier the outline plans of two relatively simple topics are given below.

On the other hand some student teachers may feel the need for even more help before embarking on a topic, and with this in mind Chapter Ten lays out an independent group topic in even greater detail.

OAK TREES—*Blackboard outline only*

Group 1 Growing an acorn

Details of an experiment to grow an acorn/Rate of germination/ Best types of soil/Parts of an acorn by name and function/ Animals that like to eat acorns/Study, size and shape of a local tree

Group 2 Care of trees

When young, staking, pruning, clearing undergrowth/Tree diseases, chemicals used to prevent disease/Method of planting trees in oak plantations/How to lop a tree/Why oak trees are lopped

Group 3 Parts of a tree

Various functions of leaves, branches, trunk, roots, flowers, and fruit/Seasonal changes in tree/Rate of growth

Group 4 Animals and trees

Animals and insects found in, on, under and around oak trees/ How the oak apple is formed/Various fungi found on and beneath oak tree

Group 5 Use of oak timber

How trees are cut, stored and seasoned/The use of oaks for charcoal burning/Use in ships (the wooden walls of England)/ Use in furniture/Various types of oak timber, especially Austrian and English oaks

Group 6 Famous oaks

A list of oaks famous in history/Charles II in an oak tree during his escape from Worcester/Oak tree at Bosworth Field, called Charles I oak/The famous oaks at Windsor Great Park/The valley of the white-leaved oak at Malvern, Worcestershire/ The Druids and mistletoe grown in oaks

ELECTRICITY—*Blackboard outline only*

Group 1 Sources of power

How various sources of power are delivered or supplied to power stations/Power sources: atom, coal, oil, water/The use of the sun to provide power in satellites

Group 2 Generating electricity

How various types of power stations work/Map of their location/Visit to local power station

Group 3 Transporting electrical power

The Grid system/How a house is wired for electric power/ Various types of battery: torch, radio, car/Power by cable between France and England

Group 4 Uses of electricity

In the home: radio, washing machines, television, power tools/ In industry: light, power tools, welding/In transport: moon vehicles and power packs/Batteries of various types/Power for small trolleys

Group 5 Natural electricity

Lightning, experiments with static electricity/Saint Elmo's fire and how it occurs

Group 6 Famous men and electricity

The experiments of Alexander Bell, Sir Humphry Davy, Marconi, Michael Faraday, Edison and Lord Kelvin

Group 7 Measuring and accounting

How we measure electricity, and how we pay for the electric power we use/The story of a day in the life of a meter inspector

Part Two | Chapter Four

The Problems of Grading Topic Work

After a brief introduction to child-centred activities in the infant and lower junior school, the following scheme of work divides topic work up into six grades.

In the first two grades the teacher is shown how she can introduce her pupils to finding various sources of information, displaying the results of their researches so that others can understand them easily and working efficiently in small groups.

The last four grades show how this work can be evolved into a methodical system for developing the children's ability to acquire fresh knowledge when working either individually or in groups.

This gradual development of topic work not only encourages children to take a personal pride in their academic achievements but, by creating opportunities for cooperation and self reliance, also makes them more confident when tackling new situations or fresh subjects in the secondary school.

General Problems

When it comes to the process of teaching young children a given subject, any scheme of work can only be regarded as an intelligent appreciation of the problems involved. If it is to be successful however, every child should feel that he is being fed fresh knowledge at a rate that allows for its easy digestion. It is important to remember that a scheme of work must be made to fit a child, rather than a child to fit the scheme.

While the following scheme is laid out in some detail, it must only be regarded as a plan from which many syllabuses can be developed which will be suited to a variety of individual requirements. Topic work, and the approach to it, is affected a great deal by a school's locality, its buildings, the type of child and the qualities of its teaching staff. Considerable thought must therefore be given to trimming, changing and remoulding the following scheme of work before its ideas can be put into operation successfully in different schools.

The importance of sequence in topic work

Because the various techniques of topic work are presented to children through the medium of many subjects, some teachers find it difficult to see any progressive sequence in this method of teaching. For this reason, specific 'aims' have been given as signposts to show how the various grades are organized throughout the school. Every effort should be made to ensure that the 'aim' of each grade is achieved before proceeding to the next grade.

Although this scheme has been broken down into six definite grades for the convenience of teachers, it should not be assumed that the children will acquire their knowledge of topics in such a disjointed manner. It is more likely that they will obtain a steady, but increasing grasp of it over a number of years. Similarly it cannot be emphasized too forcefully that it is the sequence in which the skills and techniques are taught to, and demanded from, the children which matters most.

If topic work is not approached in this way it degenerates into a series of unconnected attempts to study specific subjects, with the result that there is no overall plan throughout the school for the systematic teaching of improved techniques of learning from one topic to the next.

The topic which fails

If a teacher finds a well planned topic turning sour she should take heart, for even experienced teachers of topic work can have a 'flop' for no explicit reason.

In such circumstances the teacher should not abandon the topic, or allow it to peter out over a period of time. It is far better to take a firm grip of the problem by setting a time limit for the completion of the work. This new-found urgency to

A natural history museum was visited as part of the preparation for a topic on animals. With young children, a stimulating introduction to the subject often leads to greater interest and correspondingly better work.

Four six-year-old children co-operated to produce this model of one of the children's homes.

Children frequently work together in groups. These independent groups were each contributing separate chapters to a class topic.

complete on time sometimes pumps new life into a topic. If it does not, at least it means the whole affair is brought to a clean and tidy conclusion.

The composition of the scheme of work

To allow a quick overall view of this scheme of work it is set out below to show the basic elements of each grade. Although other types of end product can be used successfully in this graded scheme, for the sake of clarity they have not been included.

Graded topic	1	2	3	4	5	6
Contents						
Written work	10%	70%	75%	75%	60%	70%
Illustrations	90%	30%	25%	25%	40%	30%
Type of Organization						
Class work	99%	20%			50%	33⅓%
Independent Group				100%		33⅓%
Linked Group	1%	80%	100%			
Individual work					50%	33⅓%
Type of End Product						
Class Mural	100%					
Group Mural		100%				
Class Folder			100%			20%
Group Folder				100%		30%
Individual Folder					100%	50%

The foundations of a successful scheme of work

To be successful every scheme of work requires a teacher to have a sympathetic and understanding attitude of mind towards its purpose and contents. This is not always easy however, especially when the scheme is new.

Teachers must remember that graded topics are only stepping stones for helping children to create their own methods of acquiring and presenting knowledge. Similarly the various subject topics included in the scheme are there as examples only, and should not be followed slavishly. Indeed the best topics are ones which arise spontaneously due to a sudden interest among the children about a particular subject. This scheme is designed therefore, to show how such a topic should be conducted bearing in mind the age, ability, and experience of the children.

Teachers who do not think along these lines will find topics unsatisfying. Those that do, will find the work most enjoyable, and far easier than they expected.

Part Two | Chapter Five

The Infant School

The background

Before a teacher attempts topic work with the youngest class in the junior school it seems only logical that she is made aware of the basis upon which she can build such work.

While it is true to say that graded topic work cannot be undertaken in the infant school, it is also true to say that the activity methods of teaching used in these schools are so closely allied to topic work that it is nearly impossible to tell them apart. This being so, this section of the scheme of work will be confined to highlighting only those aspects of the infant school which lay the all important foundations for the children's future progress in junior school topic work.

Grouping

In the majority of infant schools, teachers are encouraged to arrange their classes so that the children spend most of their time working in small groups. To the five- and six-year-old child group work quickly becomes an accepted social arrangement within which new subjects can be learnt. This habit of co-operating with other children in order to achieve an end product is carefully fostered in infant schools and its practical applications are revealed in such activities as collecting and returning physical education equipment, the acting or miming of group plays and the building and painting of group models.

Collections

An infant teacher encourages her class to collect a wide variety of objects, because she finds that by doing so she helps them to observe more closely the world in which they live. These collections are carefully organized and result in a wide range of activities such as nature tables with clearly labelled bunches of twigs, flowers, feathers and bones, collections of unusually shaped stones or scrap books containing everything from match-box tops to Christmas cards. It must be remembered that this type of work makes an appeal to young children and by enlivening their acquisitiveness forces them to pay greater attention to their surroundings.

Encouraging curiosity

A good teacher always displays a keen desire to answer the children's questions and to discuss anything which appears of interest to them. The infant teacher cannot wait for interesting subjects to arise by accident, however, but must actively create situations and provide material about which her pupils will wish to ask questions. These question and answer periods have now become a regular feature of infant school life. One method used to provoke curiosity is to have a special shelf labelled 'Curio Corner' and provide it with such interest-arousing objects as stuffed animals or an old book, on one particular day each week. This provoking of the young child's curiosity, and active reinforcing of their natural inquisitiveness can take many forms, from nature walks to wireless programmes.

In fact the teacher who successfully implants this attitude of lively enquiry into a young child's mind gives him something which will act as an aid to learning throughout his life.

Reading and writing

The ability of the junior school entrant to read and write will probably fluctuate between non-readers, and children who can write two and three pages of good quality English. Obviously this is not the place to discuss why this happens.

It is interesting to note that some modern methods of teaching reading can result in children entering the junior school able to read and write extremely well, but unable to say the alphabet. There is no need to point out the problems that arise with dictionaries, reference books, and directories if the alphabet is unknown or badly understood.

Conclusion

Much of what amazes, delights, or horrifies us in our modern world is accepted by the young child as a normal everyday object in its natural surroundings. The telephone, car, aeroplane, television and space rocket are to the mind of the school infant familiar objects to be classified along with trees, flowers, grass, ponds, and mountains, for it has never known a world without them.

Naturally these things have an effect upon the child's mind and just as television has altered our adult horizons, so it has broadened the type of infant mind we receive into our schools. If this broadening process has been successfully nurtured in the infant school, the junior school can expect to receive seven-year-old children who have been actively encouraged to have an interest in learning.

The best type of infant school not only gives the children a high standard of reading and writing, but also inculcates group cooperation. It aims to pass on to the junior school children who have had their natural curiosity and inquisitiveness developed along constructive lines so that these two characteristics can be used as active spurs to future learning.

Lorna Ridgway and Irene Lawton in their book *Family Grouping in the Primary School** give an excellent description of the kind of infant school which is most conducive to preparing children for topic work in the junior school.

* Published by Ward Lock Educational 2nd revised edition 1969

Part Two | Chapter Six

The First Steps in Topic Work

Irrespective of their previous training in the infant school the children must, during their first few months in the junior school, be given many opportunities to experiment with the simpler aspects of topic work. The teacher must help them to adjust to their new school and establish a more individual approach to their work, reinforce any of the basic methods of topic working they have learnt in the infant school, arouse their curiosity about the world in which they live and encourage them to explore books and make discoveries for themselves.

At this stage the teacher's task, as far as topic work is concerned, is to inculcate an attitude of mind among the children which encourages them to explore a subject by accepting the responsibility for learning and discovering for themselves.

To first-year juniors the world appears to be opening out before them both physically and mentally, with the change from the infant to the junior school and their rapidly increasing ability to read books for pleasure and knowledge. The introduction of new subjects into the time table and the starting of 'out-of-school' activities such as Cubs and Brownies all excite the children's curiosity, and the good teacher will provide not only ever-changing points of interest about the classroom, but also the means of satisfying the curiosity these arouse.

Arousing and maintaining curiosity

As previously stated a good infant school will have already started the development of a child's curiosity and now the junior school must begin to exploit it so that each child is given a chance to teach himself simple facts. This process must of necessity be limited by certain factors such as each child's ability—in particular its reading ability. There is, therefore, the need for a great effort by the teacher to improve the general reading standards of the class during the first year. The books and apparatus available within the classroom and school also place a limit on this exploitation. Simple books of reference designed for children with reading ages of between 6½ and 8½ years are difficult to find and the teacher must try to augment the ones she has by recourse to the School Library Service. A third factor, which will seriously affect the scope of the work, is the external environment of the school, and in particular the amount of encouragement and help the children will receive from their parents.

This last task is the teacher's however, and not the parents', despite the fact that parents are usually most helpful. Teachers must organize a series of starting points for the children's curiosity and maintain it by providing the appropriate books and apparatus required by the children for further study. The following suggested starting points can be used and added to, as the teacher and class gain in experience.

The Nature Table

This is a common feature of most infant and lower junior classrooms and arouses considerable interest among children if it is not cluttered up with too many specimens. To prevent familiarity breeding contempt it is suggested that the nature table is used for only three short periods each term, and that each period specializes in one aspect of nature such as trees, insects, flowers, fruits, animals, birds or weather. How exploration into these subjects can be carried out is suggested on page 43. These notes will also apply to the subsequent starting points.

The Curio Corner

The word curio is here used in the sense that it applies to any object with which the majority of the children are unlikely to be familiar. It may be a strange tool used by a local craftsman, a particular piece of pottery, or a relic of some bygone age. Whatever it is the children's curiosity must be aroused enough to make them want to find out further details about it. A short class discussion, held immediately the object is presented, often helps children to consolidate their ideas while studying the object for the first time.

The 'What I found' Table

Children, especially boys, pick up and retain a wide variety of objects. Often they do not know, or care, what the object is, provided it holds an attraction for them. If the teacher holds a 'What I found' week and first arouses the children's interest by setting up a special table ready to receive the children's exhibits, she will probably be surprised by the quality and quantity of them when they arrive. What arouses curiosity in one child is quite likely to do so in another, and while not all the objects will be identified some will be. Many will require exploration in books of reference and some may even prove interesting enough to become the basis for a teacher-organized study of the subject.

The Pet Corner

If the school is equipped to cope with the children's pets for the day, or even part of the day, they can be brought to school as an interest arousing activity. When this is not possible a collection of photographs of the children's pets can be displayed. These activities can encourage children to study each other's pets, and thereby learn about the animals by seeking this knowledge from each other as well as from books.

The Latest News Place

Again space on a wall or table must be prepared and the idea of the activity explained to the children in advance. Every day, for about a week, the children must be given a chance to write a short account about some local, national or personal event of interest to them. These accounts, with any illustrations, should be displayed in one place in the classroom each day for everyone to read. An element of competition can be introduced into this work if a small reward is given for the most interesting item submitted each day.

If some children cannot write fluently enough to take part, they can be allowed to report their news verbally, for the main purpose of all this work is the encouragement of the children to look, listen and learn from the activities going on around them.

Other starting points for curiosity

A collector's table might consist of match-box tops, bark rubbings, insects, birds' eggs or stamps. The wormery and the fish tank can be used. The model corner could include all kinds from plastic kits to plasticine, and, if carefully organized over the course of a year, could provide starting points for the children's curiosity. To arouse interest by these means is not enough, each activity must give the children a good reason for seeking fresh knowledge. To this end the teacher must try to provide suitable books of reference with each subject studied.

General planning of starting points

Like all topic work, these interest arousing activities are based on the standard plan for a topic and the faint outline of each of the five stages—teacher preparation, organization of the subject, children's research and end product—should be just discernable as each one is carried out.

This means a lot of work for the teacher, but such is the nature of the school year that after a year or two have passed the young teacher should have amassed enough material and ideas to last the whole year without a disproportionate amount of effort.

Sources of reference

It is most difficult to lay down any standards for these as much will depend upon the children's reading ability and the variety of interests which will be evoked by their local surroundings. Possible sources of information are dealt with in Chapter Thirteen, but the following general points can be made about books suitable for lower juniors.

1 At this age a well labelled picture is frequently more instructive than any lengthy narrative.
2 Coloured pictures, or clear photographs, plus concise but simply worded narrative are quite acceptable to the children. Good examples are:
Looking at History, Book 1 by R. J. Unstead.

Farming by Frank Huggett.

3 Reference books of a general nature are most difficult to find but A. and C. Black and Sons' *Children's Encyclopedia*, Ward Lock's *New Wonder Book Encyclopedia*, and the *Pictorial Encyclopedia* by Sampson, Low, Marston have been found useful.

Other suitable information books are:

Your Book of . . . Series by Faber and Faber (22 books in all).

The Story Book of . . . Series by Wells, Gardener, Darton and Co (4 books).

Information Book Series by Ward Lock Educational (39 books).

Most *Ladybird Books* by Wills and Hepworth.

4 Sometimes educational journals and magazines, which are published mainly for teachers, provide articles and teaching aids which are suitable for children. For example *Teacher's World, Pictorial Education, Times Educational Supplement* and *The Teacher* are journals of this type.

5 Sometimes a book of fiction will illustrate the background to one of the more common subjects of interest to children. For example *Black Beauty* by Anna Sewell gives a young child considerable insight into the life of a horse.

All the books used with a particular subject should be grouped together and displayed as attractively as possible so that the children will be given the desire to use them. It is also sensible to take steps to see that they do so and one means of doing this is to duplicate a simple questionnaire on the subject concerned. These can be handed in at the end of a week so that good effort receives praise. See example on page 162. Another way is to display unusual views of an object showing only part of the activity or subject under study. Three- or four-line answers should be demanded stating the object's use, colour, weight, size, history, location etc. Paper and pencil should be provided along with a small post box for the finished work. Again the best answers can be suitably rewarded, or an oral lesson can be developed from this work so that every child has a chance to say what he has learnt about the subject before it is replaced by a new centre of interest.

Encouraging further exploration of a subject

Young children cannot be expected to carry out a deep exploration of a subject but they can be taught how to consider it in more than one way, and through more than one medium.

This objective can be achieved in three ways:

1 By always having a general discussion on the subject with the child or children prior to any commencement of work by them on it. Such discussions should set out to enliven the child's curiosity, suggest possible lines for further enquiry and pose questions about the subject.

2 Teaching the children to consider how objects, and subjects, appear to them when first examined, through their senses of sight, touch, hearing, smell and taste. This simple process gives them an orderly method of expanding their thoughts which can be very useful in descriptive essay work. Also it usually succeeds in emphasizing the salient points of interest in a subject.

3 Encouraging the children to study all subject matter by using each of the traditional subjects in turn. This enables each child to consider the qualities of a subject via its knowledge of English, maths, history, geography, natural history, music, art etc.

Other activities suitable for exploitation of the above techniques

The teacher can use any unusual occurrence as a starting point for providing the children with interest and they often find these good material for use in their daily diaries. For example if a bird, butterfly or mouse finds its way into the classroom, the event should be recorded in some way and the children urged to find out its name, habitat, food, etc.

The window cleaner, the school painter, an accident, the glazier, the builder, the milkman, or HMI when scrutinized in this way can provide good material for the children to investigate.

Group and individual work

Teachers may find that, as a result of their infant school training, some children tend to work in small groups on occasions. This habit should be allowed to continue, but the teacher should try to ensure that more and more individual effort is made. Although topic work is often carried out by groups of children, the main requirement of such work is that every child makes a maximum effort in order to complete adequately the task set for the group.

It is the weaker members of a class who require careful watching at this stage to ensure that they make an effort, however small or poor, to add to the common pool of knowledge being sought by the class.

Conclusion

The teacher's task during this first year is to persuade the children not to accept things at their face value, but to inquire, whenever possible, into the reasons as to why an object is as it is. By encouraging the children to speak of and write about their observations and discoveries, the teacher will sow the seeds for a more highly organized approach to topic work the following year when all these carefully established habits will be required. Indeed, one object of the entire school scheme should be to provide the children with the material and opportunities for individual exploration and discovery. By having such materials as globes, wall maps, reference books, microscopes, fish tanks, paints and paper freely available in each classroom the head-teacher will create a good environment for the growth of topic work.

Part Two | Chapter Seven

A Graded Scheme for the Junior School

Graded topic work stage 1

Type of topic: Graded/class.
Suitable for: lower juniors 7 to 8+ years.

Aim

To visit a place outside school which will arouse intense interest among the children. The object of this visit is to prepare the children to investigate a subject in such a way that:

1 The class organizes itself so that a different aspect of the subject is studied by each pair of children.
2 New sources of information are introduced such as brochures of the place visited, advertising material, posters, leaflets and trade journals.
3 The class work is finally displayed in a sequence which shows that all aspects of the subject have been studied.

Teacher preparation

The teacher is now setting out to lead the children into their first graded topic, and great care must be taken to see that it is a success. The best way of ensuring success is always good preparation which can be achieved by appreciating the problems some weeks beforehand. How to carry out an appreciation in a logical manner is given in Part Three, Chapter Seventeen. (The example quoted there is applicable to this topic.)

This preparation stage must also include:

a Choosing a subject for the topic which makes an educational excursion outside school possible, e.g. visiting a castle, museum, fire station, farm, factory, or dairy.

b Building up a collection of books, pamphlets and pictures of the subject in the classroom prior to the educational visit.

c Collecting supplies of any materials such as paper, crayons, felt markers and cardboard, which will be required for the end product of the topic.

d Preparing a duplicated booklet for use on the day of the visit (a comprehensive example appears on pages 167-74).

e Writing for any particular information required, and letters from the teacher to the School Library Service, museums and manufacturing firms asking for sources of reference and general information.

f Arousing interest in the subject by taking a few lessons on themes which are allied to the topic subject. For example, if the topic is 'Firemen' then lessons on the functions of the Police, Ambulance Service and Civil Defence Corps should be taken. These lessons will obviously arouse interest and curiosity about all the services supplied for the protection of the public, including the Fire Service.

Introduction

Sometimes a teacher is able to take an exciting event which the children have just experienced as the starting point of her topic. A road accident outside school could lead to a study of the Police or the Ambulance Service.

Usually, however, she has to introduce the subject by one of the methods listed on page 23. If possible the children should always be given the feeling that they themselves have chosen the topic subject. This can often be achieved by the teacher asking a provocative question during another lesson.

If, during a formal geography lesson on 'Farming', the teacher asks, 'What happens if a tramp sets fire to a haystack?', she can perhaps introduce the idea of a visit to the local Fire Station. Subsequent questions concerning the duties, training and homes of firemen, the types of fire fighting appliances and the whereabouts of previous local fires will soon turn the initial geography lesson into a general discussion on fire fighting and leave the children with the feeling that they have chosen their own topic subject. This activity will also give the teacher a very valuable indication as to the extent of the children's knowledge of fire fighting and the history of any local fires in particular.

Use should be made of the fact that at this age children are keen to bring things from home to show to their teacher. Frequently the teacher who assumes an air of ignorance can provoke children into bringing to school, books, toy models and even more knowledge of local interest, for there is nothing the young child likes better than to teach the teacher.

The introduction stage should last for about three or four lessons and end with the children actively seeking information about fire fighting in general.

Organization of the subject

The Educational visit

Any visit of an educational nature requires the careful planning of:

a Transport—costs, times, routes.
b Food—cost, type most suitable.
c Entrance fees and cost of guides, lectures.
d Child supervision—on and off transport, in toilets, lifts, rules for any parents present.
e Literature required—costs of guide books, pamphlets.

In this case a simple duplicated booklet should be prepared by the teacher (see example page 167) and handed out to the children on the day of the visit. The example shown was in fact prepared by a class who were experienced at topic work, but all such booklets should include:

a A timed programme of events.
b General advice on what the children should bring with them, e.g. note books, pencil, pocket money, camera, coat, etc.
c New information in précis form concerning the subject of the visit.
d An outline picture to colour.
e Advice on where to report if lost.
f Warning of any particular dangers, e.g. the feeding of dangerous animals at the zoo.

g A questionnaire to be completed before school the next day.

A well compiled questionnaire helps to ensure that the children's eyes see and record the minor details which will be required later in the classroom, and prevents the subsequent written work becoming a series of vague impressions and woolly generalizations. A list of activities which will be undertaken after the visit is over (see page 7 of the example pamphlet) also helps to ensure that the children take an active interest in the visit and it also encourages note making.

Guides

When the class arrives at the place being visited it is always advisable to use an official guide if one is available. If the guide is not very good at talking to children, it is better to ask him leading questions at appropriate moments than to attempt to paraphrase what he has said. If, however, you still feel the guide has not made a point clear to the children ask further questions until they do understand.

Organization of the subject matter

On the day following the visit, while the class still has bright visual images of the place visited, the topic should be organized so that the children can pursue their exploration of the subject further. It is still important that the children feel the whole idea is taking shape on their initiative, as indeed it will be. From her prior preparation, however, the teacher will have a good knowledge of the subject being studied, a clear picture of the finished product and a flexible scheme for seeing that every child plays his full part in the work involved.

The teacher may start this stage of the topic by suggesting to the children that they make some permanent record of their outing, and lead them on to discuss how this can best be done. These discussion sessions are important in these early class topics since they have two functions; firstly in revealing the individual interests of each child, and thereby indicating the most suitable children for each portion of the topic and secondly in allowing the teacher, with the children's help, to construct an outline plan of the topic on the blackboard. Two examples of such simple outline plans are given on page 151-2.

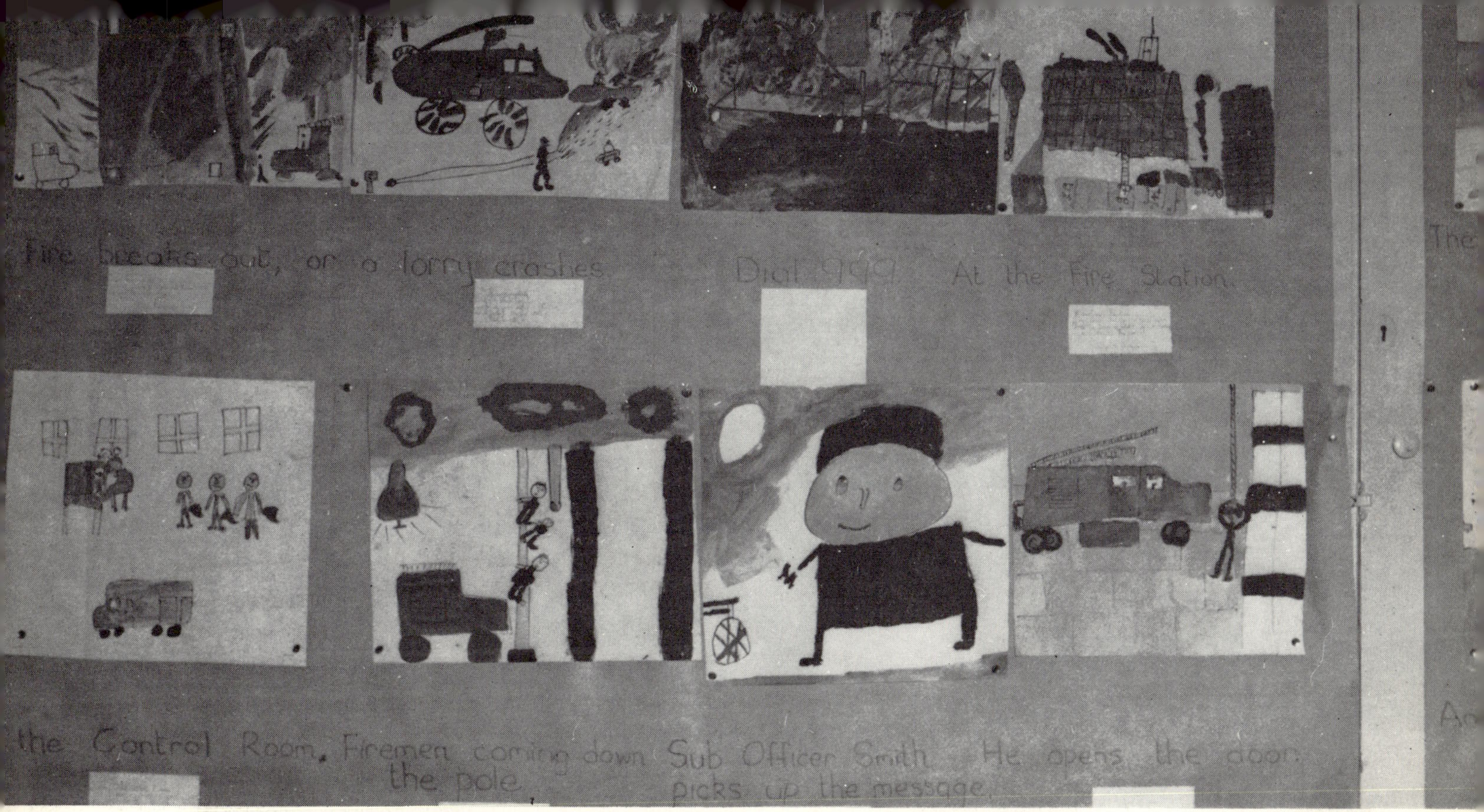

This photograph shows part of a wall frieze produced by seven-year-olds as the end product of the topic on the Fire Service described on page 49.

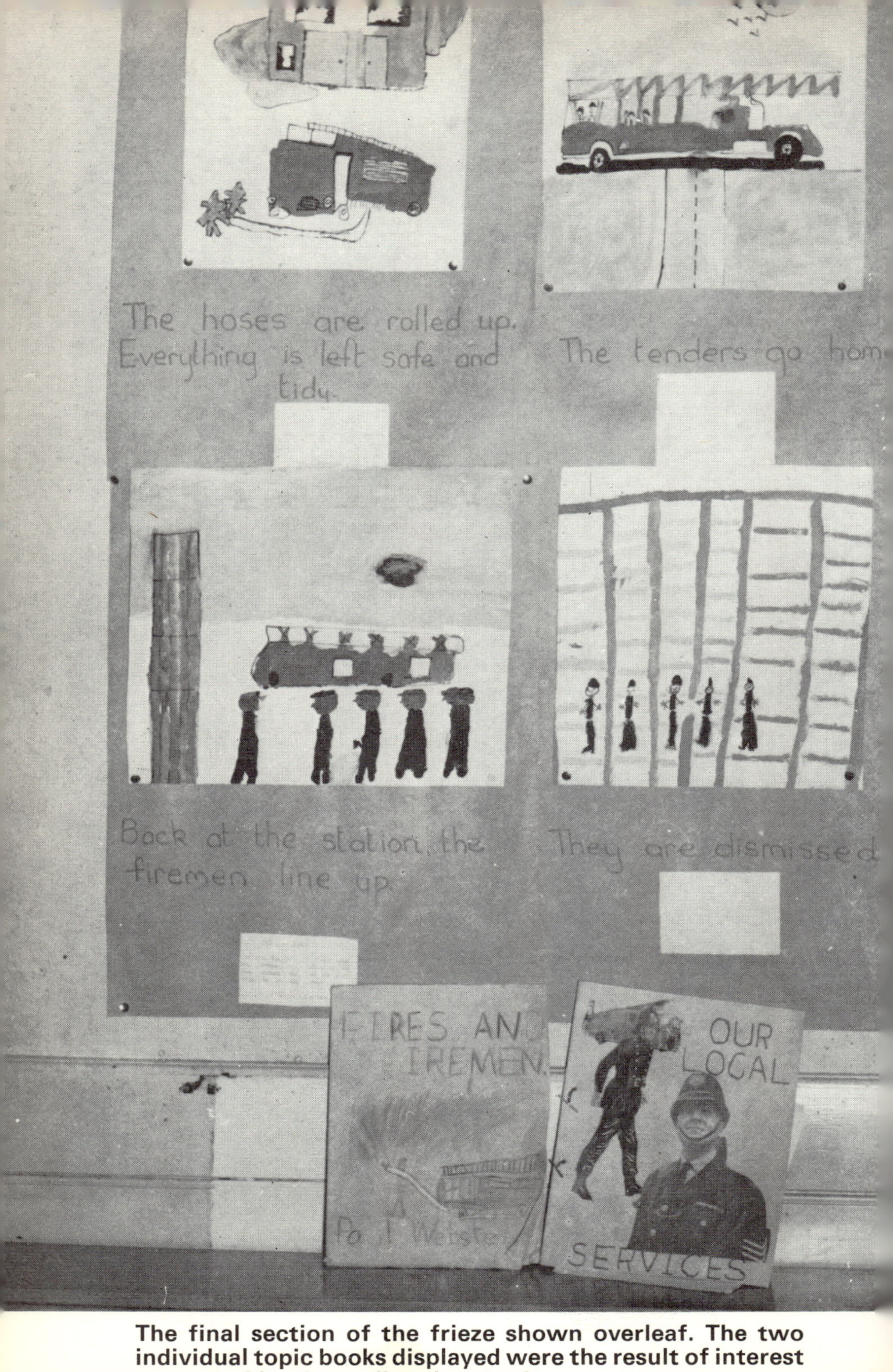

The final section of the frieze shown overleaf. The two individual topic books displayed were the result of interest generated by the earlier class topic.

With a topic on the Fire Service the following outline plan might be adopted:

1 A lorry crashes into a house.
2 People rush to help.
3 Someone smells smoke and a fire is seen.
4 Someone dials 999 and asks for the Fire Service.
5 The Fire Station control room receives the message.
6 The fireman rings the alarm bell.
7 The firemen slide down the pole.
8 The Duty Officer reads the message.
9 The officer opens the station doors.
10 The fire tender leaves.
11 The tender goes through the traffic.
12 One fireman keeps in touch with the station.
13 The tender arrives at the fire.
14 Firemen unroll their hoses.
15 The ambulance and police arrive at the fire.
16 The fire is put out.
17 The hoses are rolled up.
18 The tender returns to the station.
19 The hoses are hung up to dry.
20 The officer dismisses the men.

If this kind of outline plan is used for this grade of topic it can be seen that roughly two children will work on each section of the subject. The simplest method of finding the number of children for each group is to divide the number of subject sub-headings into the number of children in the class. For more details on grouping see Chapter Fifteen. Naturally desk arrangements, size of class, and materials available will vary extensively in each school and must have a bearing on the ultimate groupings.

Children's research

This stage will be of short duration with this type of graded topic because the children will have discovered and learnt a great deal about the subject during their education visit, and expressed their knowledge verbally. A certain amount of research will also have taken place during the introduction stage of the topic. The end product of this topic will be pictorial rather than manuscript and should not take long to produce. It is true that a certain amount of written work will be required but this will mainly describe the contents of the illustrations produced by the children. Examples of this are given on page 175; a lot of research work slows down the pace of a topic, and as these are young children, interest will be maintained better if the topic moves swiftly along.

End product

As this is the first of a series of graded topics the teacher should organize some form of wall mural as the end product of the children's work because these are easy to produce. They also make it easy for the children to gain an overall grasp of the subject when their individual contributions are displayed as one large mural. Children of this age enjoy painting and it is suggested that each pair is given a large sheet of drawing paper on which they can jointly paint a scene to illustrate their particular aspect of the subject. These paintings will portray more action if a drama or music and movement lesson on fire fighting is held beforehand. Also the children should be asked to paint all the people in their drawings about as large as the size of their own hand as this will give a feeling of continuity when the paintings are joined together for display at the end of the topic. Once this picture story is created, and displayed in sequence in the classroom, each child should be set the task of writing an account of the scene he has illustrated so that a class booklet can be made. This should contain all the written accounts, as well as photographs of the visit, pictorial illustrations of the fire service, newspaper cuttings and literature bought on the day of the visit.

If a booklet is not required the written work can be mounted beneath the appropriate painting when it is hung on the classroom wall.

Conclusion

Maintaining interest

Every opportunity should be taken to see that this topic is made an enjoyable experience for the class. Good work must always be rewarded in some way and any piece of excellent description or original poetry which has been written during the topic should also be submitted for inclusion in the school or class magazine. By doing this, and displaying the end product of the topic for all to see, the teacher gives every child a real reason for giving of his best at all times in the future.

Poor work

There is no reason strong enough to justify a teacher leaving any work out of the finished topic, if it is the honest effort of the child concerned, because the child's whole reason for participating in the topic will have been lost if such work is not displayed. The fact that bad work is shown beside good allows the children a chance to evaluate their own contribution, and encourages a desire to help the weaker members of a group when the next topic is undertaken.

All the children must be constantly encouraged to put greater detail into their illustrations, and use more vivid description in their written work, as the various grades of topic work are reached.

Time

How much time a topic takes depends on the amount of interest aroused. As a guide for planning purposes only, it is reasonable to expect this type of topic to finish within about six hours teaching time after the visit to the Fire Station.

Planning

It cannot be over-emphasized that, in these early years, good planning and adequate preparation by the teacher result in successful topics by the children. Thus, if this first graded topic is to be an enjoyable and rewarding experience for the children, the type of appreciation detailed in Chapter Seventeen must be carried out first.

Graded topic work stage 2

Type of topic: Graded/class with linked groups.
Suitable for: lower juniors, 8 to 9+ years.

Aim

To carry out a graded/class topic based on a subject which has been recently taught to the class.

This topic must give each child the experience of organizing a subject by co-operating with approximately five other children in a linked group and creating an end product the majority of which is manuscript.

Teacher's preparation

Besides carrying out the normal sequence of preparation for a topic, as described in Chapter Three, the teacher's two main problems with this topic will be to ensure that the children have been taught a good outline of the subject matter before the topic starts and to find some method of arousing the children's interest in the topic subject.

It is too readily assumed by some advocates of this type of teaching that every school can arouse interest in a topic subject by first undertaking an educational visit. Where such facilities are conveniently situated they should be exploited, but there are many schools which are so organized or sited that it is not possible for a class to undergo an interest arousing activity immediately prior to each topic.

A moment's contemplation may also convince us that it is not always desirable for such an event to take place, for a point must come in a child's intellectual development when too much time would be wasted if every topic had to be introduced by this method to achieve its successful conclusion.

It is at Grade 2, therefore, that the children are introduced to the idea of using the subject matter already taught as a basis for a topic. This not only facilitates the achievement of the 'aim' set for Grade 2, but also happens to be a natural half-way house between Grades 1 and 3.

In preparing for such a topic the teacher's very first task will be to choose a topic subject which lends itself to being discussed and taught over a period of about eight weeks without a slackening of the children's interest. The subject must also be able to be broken down into between five and nine sections, each of which are clearly separate aspects of the main subject.

Due to its natural time sequence and the availability of information at the research stage, a period in history is the simplest basis for this grade of topic.

In many primary schools the history syllabus suggests that children of this age study the Norman period, and if this is adopted as the topic subject it can be adequately covered by having linked groups on the following aspects: William I/ Castles / Churches / Villages / Hunting / Law and order / Pilgrimages/ Hereward the Wake.

Introduction

The wise teacher will allot one whole term as the most suitable unit of time for this topic because, although it will only occupy the last few weeks of term, the preceeding weeks of work will be vital to its successful conclusion.

It can be expected therefore that the teacher will spend the first part of the term giving the children an outline knowledge of the aspects of the subject listed above.

During this introductory stage the children will:

- a Study the entire Norman period under the direction of the teacher.
- b Write their own notes and collect or draw their own illustrations and they may also make a model connected with the period, such as a Saxon village or a Norman castle.
- c Become familiar with the location of the subject matter in various-reference books.
- d Read books of fiction connected with the Normans such as *Puck of Pook's Hill*, *Hereward the Wake*, *Knights Fee*, *The Shield Ring*, *Field of Senlac*, *Man with a Sword* and *Growing Up with the Normans*.

e Conceive and act short scenes associated with Norman life such as 'Trial by Ordeal'.
f Write essays using Normans and Saxons as the chief characters.

One outstanding example of this type of essay I have seen, was called 'A cabin boy goes round the world with Drake'. It took the form of a log kept by Drake's cabin boy and was original in content while being heavily flavoured with the correct historical background. A study of the Normans can offer similar opportunities, and such essays may range from: 'The diary of a lady helping to weave the Bayeux Tapestry' to, 'Why I killed William Rufus'.

About three weeks before the end of term, when the children possess a fairly firm outline of all the aspects of Norman life previously listed on page 53 this introductory stage should end.

Organization of the subject

Children of this age group still require a topic to move swiftly to a conclusion, hence the need for a reasonably long introductory stage and a short research stage with all Grade 2 topics.

Similarly the children are unlikely to respond enthusiastically to this work if the teacher quotes her own 'aims' to them as a reason for undertaking this type of topic. She must, therefore, always be ready to give them a valid reason, which they can understand, for undertaking a topic.

In this case she can point out that the term's work has to be revised and that there are a number of ways of revising a subject, including correlating it by means of a topic. She can also suggest that a well produced topic will also display to others how well they have worked during the first part of the term. She might also usefully point out that the holidays are not far away.

This fact, that the end of term is rapidly approaching, must be used by the teacher as an excuse for arousing a sense of urgency among the children. The idea of working against time often appeals to children and can be used to create both interest and a desire to complete the topic once it has started. This sense of working to a fixed deadline, with the fact that most of the research stage has already been completed during the term, should prevent a slackening of interest in the subject over a period of three weeks.

Once started the topic will conform to the normal pattern, but particular care must be taken over these three points:

1 During the discussion stage an adequate blackboard outline must be produced similar to the following:

Group I William I

Events of 1066/Types of Norman ship/Details of Bayeux Tapestry.

Group 2 Castles

Details of construction/Kinds of servants/Armour worn/Weapons used/Details of any local or well-known castle e.g. The White Tower, London.

Group 3 Churches

Details of any local church of Norman origin/Life of Norman priests/Layout and building of Norman cathedrals and monasteries.

Group 4 Saxon villages

The three-field system/Types of building/Dress of Norman and Saxon/Languages of both/Care of crops and animals/Taxes/Domesday Book.

Group 5 Hunting

Hunting of deer, boar, and hawking/Weapons used/Planting of the New Forest/Forest game laws and punishments/Death of William Rufus.

Group 6 Law and order

Trial by Ordeal and combat/Details of Hue and Cry/The Curfew/Church law/The Feudal System of responsibility to the king.

Group 7 Pilgrimages and fairs

How people travelled/Places of Pilgrimage/Dangers of travel/Why pilgrimages were made/Fair laws/Use of fairs for trade.

Group 8 Hereward the Wake

Sorting fact from fiction/Details of Saxon resistance to the Normans/Reasons why Normans required castles.

2 The formation of linked groups must be treated with great care since this will be the first occasion upon which they are

used. They should result in an equal number of children in each group, five, or six, if possible and the teacher should allow 'birds of a feather to flock together'. This last suggestion is not the most efficient or desirable method of grouping, but on this occasion it is the easiest way of providing each group with a feeling of cohesion. This is essential if 'co-operation' is to be the key word in each group's internal organization. See page 133 for details of the internal organization of group working.

3 As these children are still too young for efficient group leaders to appear, it will be the teacher's task to act in that capacity for each group. She must circulate freely among the children during the organization stage and encourage the children to experiment with new ideas for research and presentation of their subject. She must also be ready with suggestions where ideas are lacking.

As the children progress through the school, groups and grouping will present fewer and fewer problems if handled with tact.

Children's research

With the first two grades of topic work this stage is intentionally kept short so that the children's enthusiasm is maintained by the sheer swiftness of events.

To maintain momentum with this topic the teacher must actively participate in four ways:

1 By providing most of the basic subject matter required for the topic at the introduction stage.

2 By organizing all the sources of information required beforehand. In this case the children will have the knowledge they have acquired from previous lessons and their own notebooks of previous work. The sudden upgrading of their personal exercise/notebooks as a source of information can provide a sharp and useful lesson on the need for good clear notes, legibly written! They will also have previous essays based on the period concerned and a working knowledge of the available reference books and textbooks on the subject.

3 By allowing the child who is slow or backward in grasping

the requirements of this type of work to write fiction, with the appropriate historical background. Fictional writing can be part of any topic and in the later stages of individual topic work, sometimes branches out into poetry and play writing.

4 Providing the children with such aids as duplicated maps and outline drawings to complete and colour, a stock of suitable pictures, photographs, Christmas cards, old textbooks, and paper cuttings connected with the Normans. She can also help by showing filmstrips of various aspects of the period and displaying any previous class topics which children have done on this period. The desire to improve upon another class's work can be a useful stimulus.

End product

What form the topic's end product should take is perhaps best discussed at the organization stage, just after the blackboard outline has been completed.

The children always consider their group's end product extremely important and will eagerly accept advice as to how it can be improved. With this in mind, the teacher should be prepared to give guidance on how to display the end product of a topic attractively, how to store finished work during the topic, how to improve the general standard of lettering and she should also be ready to assess each group's contribution to the topic.

Since Grade 2 is a convenient point at which to teach the above techniques let us consider each of these in turn.

Displaying a topic

To succeed, the children's work must be displayed simply and attractively, and emphasize any sequence there may be in the subject. A wall mural will be most suitable for this type of topic.

On this occasion it is suggested that each linked group pastes its work on large sheets of coloured kitchen paper. A different colour should be used for each group, if possible. Once this has been accomplished the class can decide where each group's work is to be displayed on the classroom walls.

Just before this actually happens, however, the overall appearance of the work will be considerably improved if each group obtains the teacher's approval for their layout of work on the kitchen paper, before they finally paste it on.

It is pointed out that, if a wall display is not possible, a large scrap-book can be made by binding the sheets of kitchen paper together. See page 138 for details. If each group uses a different coloured paper it will make it easier to identify their contribution to the completed book.

Care of completed work

The storage of each group's completed work is sometimes a minor problem as the work proceeds. It can be overcome by using a file cover or large envelope, so that the work is kept clean before it is displayed. The custodian of the group's work should, with this type of end product, also be responsible for checking that only one side of each sheet of paper has been used.

Printing of major titles

Good printing can make poor work appear good and bad printing can make good work appear bad. In these early grades the teacher will be sensible if she standardizes the printing by undertaking to print all major titles herself. If she prints the main heading for each large sheet with a felt marker, her printing will automatically give a feeling of continuity throughout the topic when it is displayed in an orderly sequence around the classroom.

Assessment of the topic

Once the topic is completed it should not be considered to have been ended until a formal class discussion concerning its organization, progress and results has taken place.

Usually the teacher will have to ask leading questions during this discussion process to highlight what she considers to be the successful and unsuccessful aspects of each group's work.

All criticism must, of course, be entirely constructive, and the children can be helped individually if each child signs his own work with his name and age.

The introduction of this habit, at this grade, also provides the teacher with an excellent record of the progress made by each child over a series of topics.

Conclusion

The main aim of this graded topic should not be to seek very much fresh knowledge about the topic subject, but to give the children a chance to learn co-operation as they work in their linked groups.

It also enables the teacher to introduce to the children a number of useful techniques, the most important of which are:

a Producing a topic the majority of which is manuscript.
b The idea of working to a fixed time limit.
c Using fictional writing in a topic.
d The habit of signing individual work.
e Discussing and assessing the end product's good and bad points.

Teachers will of course realize that more than one Grade 2 topic will need to be carried out before all the techniques mentioned are firmly established with the class.

Graded topic work stage 3

Type of topic: Graded/class with linked groups.
Suitable for middle juniors 8+ to 10+ years.

Aim

To carry out a graded/class topic based on a subject with which the children are unfamiliar.

This topic must teach the children how to discover, select, and rewrite the information they require mainly from the textbooks available and show them how to organize and present such information in a class booklet or folder.

Teacher preparation

As usual the teacher must initially prepare the ground if the techniques to be introduced during this Grade 3 topic are to be successfully added to the children's growing knowledge of topic work.

Choice of subject matter

Again the choice of a suitable topic subject requires detailed exploration by the teacher to confirm that there is an adequate supply of information available on the chosen subject. With this grade it is extremely important that all the major sources of information only contain words which a child with a Schonell Reading Age of about 9 years can understand.

The most obvious place to look for suitable reading matter, and topic subject is among the numerous history, geography, and nature study textbooks available within the school. To take full advantage of this fact it is suggested that a period in history containing a number of people with similar characteristics or trades makes a very suitable subject for this grade of topic. Such a topic also facilitates the division of the class into a number of linked groups, each containing about six or seven children.

A topic entitled 'The Famous Sailors of Tudor England' fits

these requirements, providing group assignments on Sir Humphrey Gilbert, Ferdinand Magellan, Sir Richard Grenville, John Hawkins, Sir Walter Raleigh, Henry Hudson, Sir Martin Frobisher and Sir Francis Drake.

Alternative topic subjects include 'Inventors of the Industrial Revolution', 'Famous Airmen of the Twentieth Century', 'Nineteenth-Century Explorers', 'Great Scientists' and 'Britain's Trees'.

See page 154 for an outline plan of another suitable subject.

Preparation of information sources

With this type of graded topic the teacher must supply the children with many textbooks, library books and filmstrips connected with the Tudor period, maps of voyages made by Tudor sailors and large political and physical maps of the countries they visited and discovered. She must also provide duplicated outline maps for the children to complete, in particular outline maps of the World and a number of historical and general knowledge encyclopedias. She should also consider obtaining, or supplying, plastic scale models of the ships used and visiting, or obtaining material from, the Greenwich Maritime Museum or the Science Museum.

Introduction

Provided that all previous topic work has been carried out successfully, an elaborately planned introduction to this topic will not be necessary because by this age the children will be keen to undertake such work.

While the teacher should now persuade the children that it is time that they accepted more responsibility for the actual organization of the topic, she should do so by phrasing her introductory words in such a way that they present a challenge to the children. For example it is better to start a sentence, 'Do you think you have grown up enough to . . .' or, 'See if you can show me how you would . . .' than to give a direct instruction or explanation. Provided the children feel they have a good chance of attaining their goal, the teacher's challenge will usually be accepted with enthusiasm.

Obviously any of the methods listed in Chapter Three can be

used for introducing this grade of topic, but from now on the pleasure the children get from this type of work should be enough to give them a desire to produce a successful end product.

This does not mean that if a novel or exciting approach to the work is available it should be ignored, but only that it is not quite so important as in the past.

As this grade of topic requires the children to attempt their own exploration of the subject matter, the introduction stage will be considerably shorter than in Grades 1 and 2, and may only consist of a general lesson, talk, or filmstrip on the Tudor sailors and in particular their trading, fighting, and shipbuilding activities. The children should be allowed to undertake a short investigation of the subject prior to the next stage of the topic and to agree upon the shape and form of the end product.

Organization of the subject

Let us assume that prior to the formation of linked groups the teacher allows the children about an hour to investigate the subject matter and discover which of the Tudor sailors already mentioned is of personal interest to each of them.

Grouping

Grouping can now take place mainly on the basis of personal choice. Exactly how this is achieved is given in detail in Chapter Fifteen.

Introduction of potential Group Leaders

During the formation of each topic group the teacher must arrange matters so that a potential group leader is included in each group. These children should be capable of filling the roles of natural leaders within their respective groups on this occasion. In later topics they will be expected to emerge as group leaders responsible for all the aspects of their group's work. For a list of their duties see page 70.

Provided these potential group leaders accept a little responsibility for their group's behaviour the number of groups requiring help and supervision by the teacher should be reduced to a manageable proportion. For example a class of forty-two children can be split into six groups of seven children. If two of these groups become fairly self sufficient, the teacher has only four groups left to help.

Organization of the subject matter

Until this grade the class has combined to draw up an overall outline of the subject on the blackboard as the examples on pages 49 and 55.

The establishment of an organized and logical approach to a subject must now become the responsibility of each group, and the teacher must assist this process by providing each group with an encyclopedia containing a compact account of the character being studied and a number of textbooks containing the additional information required for a comprehensive study of the subject. She must also ask each group to show and explain to her their outline plan before they embark on the research stage of the work and she must ensure that every child in each group is responsible for at least one specific part of the group's researches.

Children's research

This stage will take up more and more time as each new graded topic is tackled, but in this case, with about seven children in each group, the work should proceed fairly quickly since the groups are large.

In any topic the research stage is the most difficult of all for achieving successful results, and it is in Grade 3 that the children will first be expected to discover, select, and rewrite information without a great deal of help from the teacher. They will have been prepared for this task however by having seen the teacher carry out this stage during the course of previous graded topics, because they have always helped with this process whenever possible. The teacher will have selected and distributed to each group at least seven or eight relevant textbooks immediately prior to the commencement of the research stage so that each group will have a ready made pool of knowledge into which they can plunge.

Copying of textbook material

With the introduction of textbooks as the major source of information there is a tendency for the children to copy lengthy extracts. All children appear to pass through this phase of copying textbooks, and it should always be discouraged because it frequently implies that only one source of information has been consulted and that the copied paragraphs are not truly understood by the child concerned.

To counteract copying the children should be persuaded to read widely on a subject so that, before they describe it in their own words, they obtain the vivid mental pictures they require. How wide reading can be encouraged is dealt with more fully in Chapters Twelve and Thirteen.

Inter-group cooperation

Quite often one group's research will reveal information of great interest to another group. While the interchange of information has been encouraged during previous topics the subject matter of this one makes it an ideal occasion for the teacher to emphasize the importance of this habit. It should be forcefully pointed out that if everyone helps his neighbour, in the long run all must benefit.

End product

At the introduction stage the class should have decided the form of the topic's end product. So far topic work has been confined to making murals, and the children will be ready for a change. The idea of writing a book appeals to children of this age, and one entitled 'The famous sailors of Tudor England' will allow each group to contribute the life story of one personality in the form of a chapter.

When pointing out the advantages of a book over a mural as an end product the teacher should mention that it is a compact and portable method for containing their work which can be easily retained as a handy source of reference and can also be loaned to other classes for reading. She should also point out that a number of well produced topic books can, over the course of time, make a very interesting reading library.

Shaping each group chapter

A short discussion can quickly reveal that in this topic each chapter can have a common outline and framework. Obviously their contents will differ with each sailor, but each group should adopt a similar pattern of presentation. For example one outline which has been found useful is:

Page 1	Title page.
Page 2	Names and ages of the children who wrote it.
Page 3	A short account of how the work was carried out. (Not more than a page.)
Page 4	A picture, drawing, or photograph of the subject being studied.
Page 5	A list of contents with page numbers for reference.
Next pages	Details of the subject compiled in a logical sequence. (Date order is easiest.)
Last page	List of books, filmstrips and useful addresses for future reference.

Size of topic book

As a book is to be the final product of this topic, quarto-sized paper is suggested as the most manageable size and one which allows good clear illustrations to be made. Some children seem to have a natural desire to fill a page and quarto helps to encourage them to write as much as possible.

Assembling the end product

Once each group has completed its allotted chapter the teacher will need to anticipate the problem of sorting and presenting the completed book. The final touches, such as a cover, and a full list of contents should be allocated to children who will finish them quickly, for everyone will be anxious to see and read the final product.

Suggestions as to how the book should be covered and joined together are given in Chapter Sixteen.

Assessment and testing of the topic

Once every topic is completed the class should discuss the problems that have been encountered, or the new ideas that have been discovered. No hard and fast rules can be laid down for this activity but teachers should see that with this graded topic the printed headings have been standardized throughout the book and that the writing, which need not be standardized, is clear and easy to read. An excessively high standard of identical writing usually reveals two things. First that considerable copying from textbooks can be found in the contents of the topic and secondly that a great deal of time has been wasted in teaching handwriting which could have been more usefully employed in topic research. Provided each child writes a clear, clean hand which portrays its own character the end product itself will have character.

The teacher should also make sure that illustrations and maps are clear and adequately titled and that descriptions of personal experiences are prominently placed. A description of a child's visit to the replica of the *Golden Hind* at Brixham is likely to be far more vivid and instructive than any knowledge obtained from books.

Testing

While the main object of a graded topic is to improve topic techniques it is also intended to teach a part of a subject. As this is so the teacher should attempt to assess how much has been learnt. An example of a questionnaire suitable for this topic is given on pages 164-6.

Conclusion

To be successful all Grade 3 topics should, when finished, have taught the children:

a How to extract the knowledge they require from simple books when working on their own.
b How to compare dates, and arrange facts in a logical order when working as a group.
c How to cooperate so that relevant information is passed to, and used by, the correct group.
d How to accept more responsibility for all aspects of the work.

Graded topic work stage 4

Type of topic: Graded/class with independent groups.
Suitable for: top juniors 9+ to 11+ years.

Aim

To undertake a graded class topic similar to a Grade 3 topic but using independent groups and a less well defined subject.

During this topic emphasis must be placed on three aspects of the work. Firstly group leaders must be introduced, given responsibility and have their functions defined. Secondly groups must now be made more self sufficient and thirdly a deliberate attempt must be made to widen the scope of topic work by actively incorporating other subjects on the school syllabus such as art, music and drama.

Teacher preparation

Although two more advanced grades of topic work are possible in the junior school, this grade is the maximum standard of attainment which can be expected of some children under eleven years of age.

The teacher will still be required to plan a topic carefully and provide a wide range of information sources in advance. With a wide ranging subject such as a period in history, a nationalized industry, a particular type of music, or school of painting, the teacher's task becomes quite extensive, especially when, as in this case, a deliberate attempt is made to widen the scope of the work.

Introduction

At this age no carefully contrived introduction to the work is necessary, for by now, topic work should have become a well established method of learning. If a class is backward, or without previous topic experience, an attractive introduction will of course still be required. Should this happen however, the teacher would be well advised to seriously consider undertaking an easier grade of topic.

What form the end product of this topic should take must be considered at this stage. A quarto-sized group booklet is a most suitable choice. It helps to foster a feeling of independence and self-sufficiency because it makes each group responsible for its own end product. Group booklets also give greater opportunities for participation by all the children in the final stages of organization and presentation and make it easier for each group to produce a similar looking topic because all the work will be presented by each group on a standardized size of paper.

Organization of the subject

Preliminary investigation of the subject matter

Once the scope and content of the subject have been established by means of a short class discussion, the class should spend about two hours on a preliminary investigation to discover the availability of information, the most important aspects of the subject, the personal interest of each child and any logical order there may be in the subject.

Establishing order

With historical subjects date order is always the easiest to establish. With geographical subjects their location, or the seasons, provide order. With art and music, personalities, or a historical period give a logical sequence. The sequence of production usually decides the steps required for a logical investigation of an industry.

Whatever the subject, order should be quickly established, and it is a good idea to enlist the children's help in displaying the main features of a subject logically on the blackboard. This should therefore be done immediately after the preliminary investigation is complete.

This process always reveals how well the teacher has prepared the subject for she should have already made her own outline plan of how the subject can be broken down into suitable amounts for study by small groups of children. When she is preparing this outline it is a good idea to arrange for one or two of the subjects to be easier than the rest so that the weaker members of the class can be encouraged to work on them.

Grouping

As children become increasingly familiar with topic work so the groups should become smaller, and by this grade five children to a group should allow an adequate investigation of a subject to be undertaken.

When forming the groups the teacher's tact and patience must again come into play, for she will be faced with the task of including a potential group leader in each group, as well as allocating correctly the limits of each group's responsibility for the work, i.e. seeing that the main subject is broken down in such a way that each group has adequate scope for its talents. She must also ensure that the weaker groups are given the easier tasks and she should point out to each group that with this topic they will be working on subjects which will have very little in common with other groups and can therefore expect very little help or cooperation from them.

This can be illustrated if we take a period in history and draw up a possible outline plan such as may be made by the class for this type of topic.

The Stuart Period

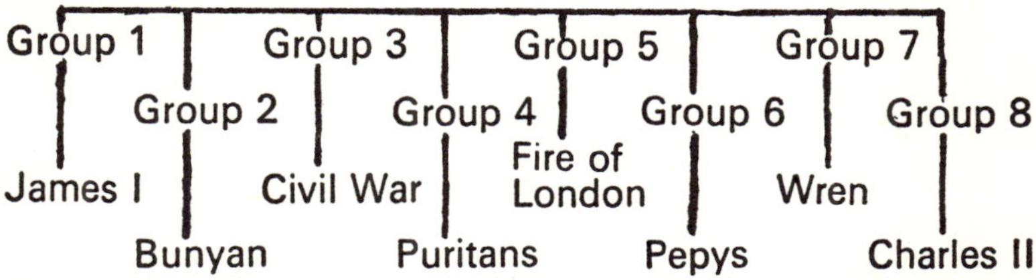

See pages 156 and 157 for other outline plans of topics suitable for this grade.

Group leadership

The very nature of each group's subject should demand self-sufficiency from the group itself with regard to all aspects of the work. Snags and differences of opinion will occur and teachers should not be surprised by this, for the children will take time to see the problems involved. Harmonious working automatically demands a certain degree of group leadership. Such leadership evolves because it is simpler to channel all problems through one child for explanation and help by the teacher. When this occurs groups seem to turn quite naturally to the right child to act as group leader. If it does not happen then the group can quickly vote for who shall have the task.

While the teacher has been planning this move for some time it helps to put the idea across if the words 'group leader' are not mentioned prior to this grade, as in actual fact this is the first time that a 'group leader' has any independent function.

The group leader's tasks should include:

a Being the liaison link between the group, the teacher and other groups.
b Helping to promote self discipline and hard work by personal example.
c Collection and care of completed work.
d Accepting the responsibility for organizing the group once work starts.
e Organizing and presenting the group's end product.
f Persuading everyone to accept a decision made by the majority of the group.
g Seeing that all the work involved is fairly allocated to the various members of the group.

These are only the main zones of responsibility and group leaders should also be expected to undertake other responsibilities from distributing writing materials to discovering new sources of information. Briefly their role can be described as one who is the 'servant of all and the master of none'.

With experienced group leaders it may be possible to allow them to experiment with the task of allocating the various aspects of the group subject. For example with a group investigating 'The Fire of London 1666', the group leader might break the subject down so that each member of the group is responsible for only one of the following aspects of the main subject: London's appearance before the fire/Events during the fire/Damage caused/Rebuilding afterwards/The fire fighting methods employed and developed afterwards/St Pauls before and after the fire.

The allocation of work is a difficult problem and the teacher will usually help by suggesting suitable subsections of the main subject to individual children. She should however, always try to allow the children to solve their own problems and deal with each group through its leader, so that each group develops a collective sense of responsibility for the work.

Children's research

As the children become more proficient at seeking, selecting, absorbing and recording knowledge, so this research stage becomes more important and takes longer to complete. At this grade a certain amount of help will still have to be given by the teacher as each group is seeking information about the main subject at the same time. The major problem here is that a large number of books are required for each group to cover its subject, and the children usually find that no one book or chapter groups together all the information they require. The teacher must act as a liaison agent and encourage each group to keep an eye open for items of knowledge of interest to other groups. If this is done successfully it is surprising how quickly the books available are sorted to the groups who require them and how freely books containing useful chapters are passed from child to child after use.

End product

Widening the scope of the topic

As each group will produce its own booklet at the end of this topic the teacher must attempt to widen the scope of the work and link it more directly with other subjects and lessons taking place in the children's lives. This can be done by:

- a Introducing the making of linocuts as a source of illustration—head and shoulder prints come out very well.
- b Making simple models from plasticine or clay.
- c Weaving booklet covers and sewing titles on them.
- d Printing curtains with linocuts of historical personalities or animals.
- e Sewing felt pictures concerned with the events or subject of the topic.

f Painting large murals to tell a story, after the style of the Bayeux Tapestry.
g Mimes and plays based on the subject of the topic.
h Playing music of a historical period being studied, or listening to any musical pieces of a descriptive nature if they are appropriate.

Improving the quality of the topic

Alongside these activities come three others concerned with improving the qualities of presentation within the topic itself. Firstly a demand for better standards of lettering, writing, and drawing. The use of felt pens and lettering pens should be encouraged. It is particularly helpful if teachers discuss the use of lettering and then display examples in the classroom showing how each type of lettering is best suited to the function it has to perform. Then the order of presenting the work within the folder, or booklet, should be clarified with the children so that each group's work is given a feeling of unity with the others when they are all placed together. How, and when to use pen, pencil, crayon, and ball-point pen always requires special clarification.

Thirdly, just as a subject can be broken down into subsections suitable for group study, so too can simple pictorial diagrams be produced which illustrate the contents of each of the subsections.

Assessment and testing

This particular type of topic really begins to test how well the children have grasped the principles of topic work and where their weaknesses lie. After assessing the end products of the first Grade 4 topic attempted, it may well be that the teacher will decide that a number of Grade 4 topics will have to be carried out before the group leaders are capable of organizing a group successfully.

With some classes Grades 5 and 6 may never be attempted within the junior school, but this should be regarded as the exception rather than the rule.

Testing

With this Grade should come a greater demand for the children to acquire more detailed knowledge of the subject they have studied. Testing this knowledge will be difficult as each group will have been working on a different subject. An inter-group verbal 'What do you know?' competition organized and scored by the teacher often emphasizes this point for future topics.

Conclusion

Once the children have mastered all the topic techniques so far suggested in this scheme of work, it has been found that with fairly intelligent children there appears to be no limit to the subjects which can become the basis for a topic.

Besides achieving its stated 'aim' this grade should have helped to smooth, polish and complete earlier techniques and to promote greater individual responsibility so that the children have been led towards individual topic work.

It is therefore a good idea to introduce individual topic books after this grade has been completed. This will allow the children to make mistakes and discoveries for themselves, which will make them more receptive to suggestions contained in Grade 5. Individual topic work is the aim of Grade 5 but the children can obtain a great deal of help from the suggestions given in Chapter Eight if they wish to attempt an individual topic book before Grade 5 is reached.

Graded topic work stage 5

Type of topic: Graded/individual.
Suitable for: top juniors 10+ to 11+ years.

General comment

This grade is in the nature of a formal exercise to prepare children for undertaking the type of individual topic described in Chapter Eight. Of necessity it creates an entirely artificial atmosphere in which to carry out an individual topic, and results in much of the children's work being carefully directed. The children must be given adequate scope for expressing their own individuality however, especially during the research stage, and in their method of presenting their topic's end product.

Aim

For each child to have the satisfaction of producing a good individual topic under the direct guidance of the teacher.

Although this work will be mainly a practice exercise on individual topics it is intended that each child will be responsible for presenting in his own words the information discovered by the class as a whole, that the weaker members of the class will gain enough self-confidence to undertake future individual topics on their own and that everyone will discover how their previous attempts at individual topics can be improved.

Teacher preparation

Many teachers may feel that their own upper juniors are too competent at topic work for there to be any necessity for this grade of topic to be undertaken. Experienced teachers have found that this is rarely so and that the great majority of classes require a teacher's help with their first individual topic.

When preparing for this topic the teacher must choose a subject which can be conveniently divided up into a number of short stages so that all the children can proceed through the topic at the same rate. The life of some famous person usually provides very suitable subject matter for this type of topic.

The teacher must ensure that the supply of books about the chosen subject is large enough to allow for a simultaneous research of the subject by the entire class and she must herself have previously acquired a wide knowledge of the subject matter, which she will require when she organizes an outline of the subject on the blackboard from the information discovered by the children during the research stage.

Introduction

The teacher should first explain that she wishes to show the class how to organize an individual topic. The fact that some of the class will have already experienced difficulties while experimenting with individual topics will be enough introduction to this grade since these children will be fairly competent topic workers and quite willing to learn new techniques.

Organization of the subject

As has already been mentioned the subject matter of this type of topic must be capable of being studied one stage at a time. For example the life of Captain James Cook is ideal for this grade of topic as it divides itself up into chapters on: Cook's early life/His time in Canada with General Wolfe/His first and second voyages/His third voyage and death.

Similarly Samuel Pepys can be studied under the following chapter headings: England during Pepys' childhood/Pepys and the Navy/Pepys' family, dress, and entertainments/London before 1666/The Plague and Great Fire as seen by Pepys.

The life of Florence Nightingale can become a study of the world in which she lived by dividing it into chapters on: Life in an English village of 1830/The various styles of dress Florence wore during her lifetime/The various forms of transport she would have used/Life in hospital before 1850/The Crimean War/How Florence Nightingale improved hospitals from 1860 onwards.

When considering other subjects for this grade the teacher may find it possible to divide them into early life, family, outstanding events and death. In the case of insects and plants, their life cycle provides suitable material for chapter headings. With many geographical subjects the subject matter can be conveniently considered under the headings of the four seasons of the year.

Children's research

The research for each chapter is only undertaken by the class as each one is reached. Since by this grade the children are good at discovering any information they require, this task can be left entirely to them provided the teacher has previously ascertained that sufficient sources of information are available.

With every child seeking the same information, the most suitable books are quickly discovered. The sources must, however, be organized and this can best be done by the teacher listing them in chronological order on the blackboard in the following manner:

DATE	EVENT	BOOK
1854	Crimean War	Kingsway History Book 4
1855	Scutari Hospital	Lady with the Lamp
1856	Victoria Cross	Pictorial History Book 4

Once all the sources of information for each chapter are listed on the blackboard it gives every child a firm foundation upon which to build up its own description of events required for that stage. It will be seen that although knowledge is collectively discovered, the responsibility for its collation and presentation becomes that of the individual child.

End product

It is realized that each child's finished product will be very similar but individuality of presentation can be achieved by encouraging each child to present the contents of each chapter in his own way and to use individual styles of writing and various methods of illustration. A sense of competition to devise the most eye-catching front cover for the child's personal topic folder can also help stimulate individuality.

The teacher can assist this topic by providing each child with a simple folder cover (foolscap size) for the protection of its work, duplicating any outline maps which may be required and giving instructions on the making of map keys and by providing a wide range of art materials and facilities.

Conclusion

Most children obtain a great sense of achievement from completing an entire topic of their own. This applies especially to the weaker members of the class who gain more confidence in their ability to carry out future individual topics, as they have been responsible in this grade for completing the end product of each stage for themselves.

It is also very important that this grade is undertaken before the class proceeds to Grade 6 because it will require them to work independently if they are to complete successfully their group assignments.

Graded topic work stage 6

Type of topic: Graded/class with independent groups containing individual topics.
Suitable for: upper junior and lower secondary children 10+ to 13+ years.

General comment

A Grade 6 topic is designed so that while very child is required to work on his own subject, he also makes an important contribution to the work of the entire class. The final goal of all graded topics is to give children the ability to teach themselves, but this is unlikely to be achieved until their final months in the primary school, or the first years of their secondary school life.

Before attempting this grade the children should be proficient at both 'group' and 'individual' topics, and this further emphasizes the importance of carrying out Grade 5 carefully.

Aim

To undertake a graded class topic using four or five independent groups. Each independent group assignment will require an investigation into only one aspect of the class topic subject and force each group to produce its own end product, e.g. a booklet. The assignments will be capable of sub-division into individual topics so that every child is working on his own to produce one complete chapter for the group's end product. This topic will invite the children to rely heavily on sources of information outside the school, e.g. correspondence with Museums, Trade Associations, Learned Societies, etc.

Teacher preparation

Once the teacher has planned the outline of the topic there is very little preparation requiring extra care except the location and collection of various addresses where information may be acquired.

Introduction

During their last few months in the junior school most children seem to boil over with an enthusiasm for seeking fresh knowledge, and trying out new ideas. As this is so, the introduction of a new form of topic is most unlikely to arouse any opposition. In fact it is quite likely that with an intelligent class of children, they may quite naturally adopt this form of topic work for themselves.

Organization of the subject

This topic gives the teacher an excellent opportunity to introduce the idea of writing letters to various associations, societies, museums and manufacturers so that they become the major source of information on the subject being studied. Only one letter should be written to each source of information on behalf of the whole class since many letters asking for the same information will be time wasting for the recipient and will tend to destroy the goodwill of such people.

This work should be carried out as the first stage of the topic so that the information is available when the research stage is reached.

Letter writing

As these letters are an integral part of their topic the children should be taught to make an exact copy of each letter they write, date stamp and file every reply they receive and include all their correspondence in the final end product.

The importance of keeping a copy of their own letters is brought home to the children on those occasions when they find themselves entering into regular correspondence with some outside body.

This seeking of knowledge outside the bounds of the school costs both time and postage, but it should be made a feature of this final topic because this is the way much of the information the children require for all their individual topics can be obtained.

Choice of the topic's subject matter

The subject of 'Farm Animals in Britain' makes a good basis for a Grade 6 topic.

Five independent groups can be formed, and each given one of the following assignments: Horses and ponies/Cattle/Pigs and goats/Chickens, ducks and geese/Sheep. Each of these group assignments can be sub-divided into chapters which are individual topics dealing with: Food/Diseases/Products/ Costs/Characteristics of various breeds/Buildings required and design problems/Areas where the animals are found and why/ Machinery used/Markets and shows/History of the animal's development. These individual topics give ample opportunity for each child to explore their subject without feeling too restricted.

Teaching of self-reliance

A feeling of independence and self-reliance can be further encouraged among the children if the teacher makes every effort to deal with each child's problems only through the elected leader of the group.

The preliminary discussion of the group's assignment and subsequent allocation of work into individual topics should now become the group leader's responsibility.

The form of the end product

What form the topic's end product will take can be agreed by the entire class discussing and agreeing the matter prior to the start of work or by the group leaders agreeing a method among themselves after their groups have made a preliminary reconnaissance of the subject.

Children's research

By the time this grade is reached it is quite likely that the children will have completed some individual topic books similar to those described in Chapter Eight.

If this is so, the teacher will find that they have a very good working knowledge of many sources of information both inside and outside school.

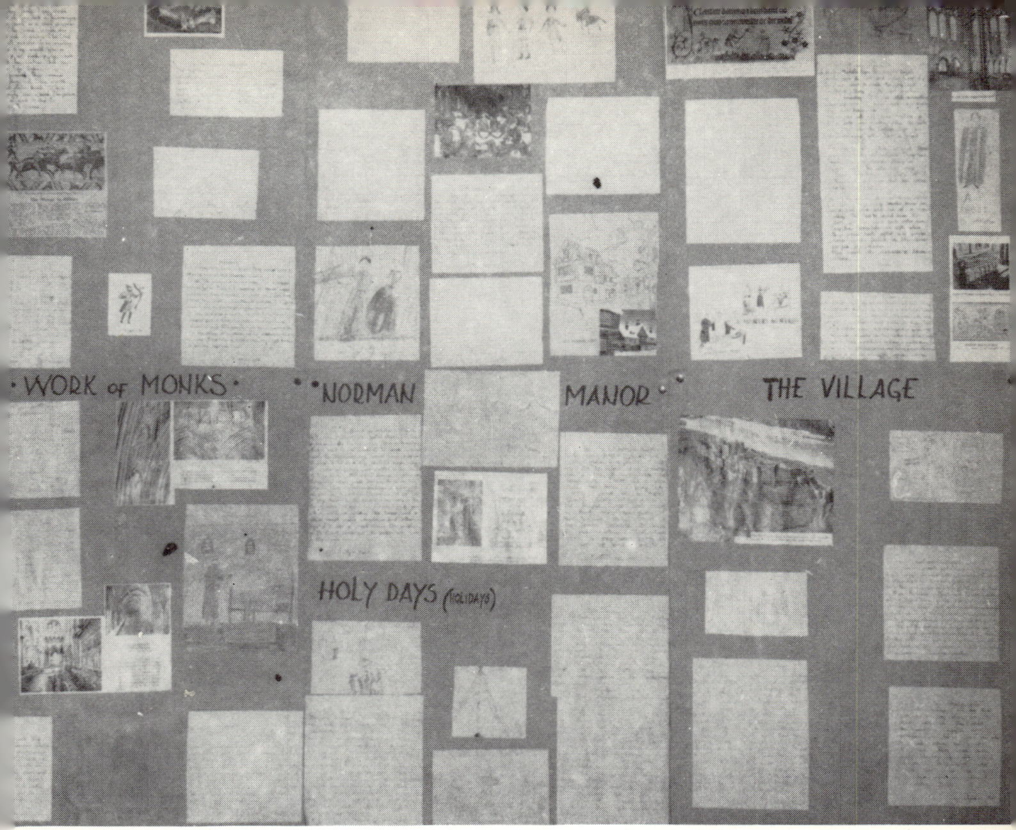

This large wall display was the end product of a Grade 2 topic on the Normans.

Five group topic folders produced for a Grade 4 topic on the Stuarts.

This frieze accompanied a Grade 3 topic on the life of Shakespeare. The illustrations were done by the children, the lettering by the teacher.

A nature study topic showing how prepared lists can assist children in displaying the information they have collected.

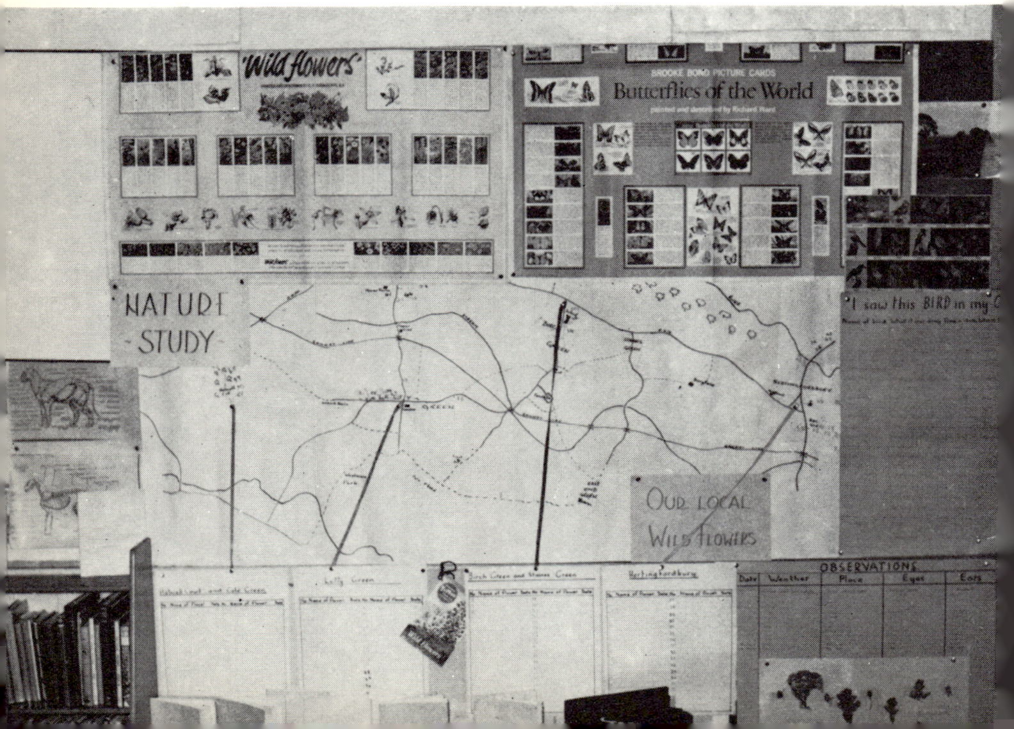

The telephone

When the appropriate moment arrives the children should be made aware of the usefulness of the telephone as a means of obtaining a quick answer to a vital question which is holding up their work.

Educational visits

At all ages children benefit from well planned visits to places of interest, but this grade of topic often makes a visit to a particular section of a local museum, farm or factory a very rewarding experience for upper juniors.

If such visits can be arranged so that only small 'group-sized' parties are taken, the children seem to obtain even greater benefit from their experience.

A shortage of suitable books

It is quite possible to carry out a Grade 6 topic without using many books dealing with the subject matter, provided it is carefully chosen.

If this is attempted it means that every child in the class must write away asking for information before the work can proceed very far.

One school applied this technique to a study of Australia. The independent group assignments were: Western Australia/ South Australia and Northern Territory/Queensland/New South Wales/Victoria and Tasmania.

The individual topics contributing to each independent group assignment were: History of the State/Wild life and flora/ Climate/Geographical structure and minerals/Its people/ Transport systems/Medical services/Holiday centres and sports/ Industries/Schools.

The information required was obtained mainly from three sources: Australia House, and various large banks and firms having branches in Australia; the children's relations in Australia—the topic was suggested by the fact that seven of the children had relations living in Australia—and a school in Sydney. Before writing to the school the children made a scrap-book containing wild flowers, cigarette packet tops, match-box tops, insects, used postage stamps, used tickets, labels of every sort, picture post cards of their town, and letters describing their lives in Britain. This scrap-book was forwarded to the Australian school just before Christmas, and a similar book was received just before the following Whitsun, which finally sparked off the children's desire to study Australia in greater detail.

From all these activities an overwhelming supply of literature, illustrations, periodicals, maps and guide-books was received. These were formed into a pamphlet library so that the most up-to-date details on Australia were available for everyone.

End product

This topic like the one on Farm Animals of Britain, produced five thick booklets (13 by 9 inches) containing about forty pages of written work. All the correspondence and other material obtained on Australia was included in a separate section at the end of each group booklet. The outside cover of each book was decorated by cutting out the more colourful advertisements obtained and sticking them on.

More outline plans suitable for Grade 6 topics are given in Appendix One.

Conclusion

Being released from the normal sources of information required for a topic such as school library, filmstrips, home, etc., gave the children a feeling of great satisfaction and enough self-confidence to try more ambitious subjects in their individual topic books.

Writing letters and maintaining a continuous correspondence with various sources of information outside school became a natural and everyday occurrence, instead of an unusual and artificially forced process.

Part Three | Chapter Eight

Individual Topic Work

For the teacher the main difficulties associated with individual topic work can be very simply classified under the three headings of why? when? and how? Let us therefore first consider the reason why such work should be undertaken and state clearly its aim.

Aim

To give each child an opportunity to practise and experiment with the techniques already learnt from graded topics in order to produce, unaided, a topic on a subject of his own choice.

Why

During the process of achieving this 'aim' the child should be guided continually towards complete self-reliance when dealing with the problems involved in undertaking an individual study, and, by experimenting, to form a topic style of his own. Thus it can be seen that this type of work can be undertaken and run parallel to the last few stages of the main course of graded topic work so that the children are given a means of undertaking a topic in their own way and at their own speed.

When

It is not possible to suggest a specific age for the commencement of individual topics for the question of when they should be introduced depends entirely on the ability of each child to grasp the underlying principles involved in such work. Usually this occurs with intelligent children at about the age of eight or nine and frequently coincides with the age at which they attain complete mastery over the problem of reading for information.

There also comes a time when children become so competent at writing a good 'Daily Diary' that the process becomes boring because it is of little practical use to either the child or teacher and individual topic work can therefore be introduced to take its place.

Individual topics, then, can be introduced when a child has gained enough experience of topic work to enable him to produce a reasonable amount of work in the time available each day and when the child's ability is such that he is capable of learning by making his own mistakes without being discouraged.

If thirty minutes per day are allocated for this work, the average output by the normal child will be about three pages of written work a week, but the main asset of such work will be that it will give the child a chance to put theory into practice and give the teacher a clear indication as to how well the techniques of topic work are being learned.

At this point therefore it is fair to ask how individual topics can be used to improve the general standard of topic work undertaken in other subjects for, if they are to run an independent and parallel course to the main scheme of graded topic work, it is obvious that they are a very convenient method of augmenting and revising such work. They can also be used to introduce many of the minor and less important problems connected with presentation and choice of subject matter.

How

The carefully controlled individual topic outlined in Grade 5 (page 74) should be carried out so that the children can attain confidence in their abilities before they undertake a similar topic on their own. The actual amount of time to be allocated to these individual topics depends upon how the school is organized and the amount of enthusiasm the children have for such work. If no time limit is set for completion of the work and about thirty minutes per day are allocated to it in school, the children should be encouraged to continue the work at home. This method has many advantages, not the least of which being that it often results in the parents taking a considerable interest in the whole process.

Sometimes it is quite surprising how much difficulty a child has in finding a suitable subject around which to weave his topic and the teacher should try to approve each subject selected before a serious start is made on the work. No attempt should be made to alter the child's choice of a subject but sometimes it is advisable to suggest the angle from which the subject should be approached. For example, a child wishing to do a topic on wild flowers should be persuaded to deal mainly with those wild flowers found in his own locality.

The grading of subjects

The following list is graded to show the categories into which subjects can be classified in increasing order of difficulty. In each case some examples of subjects actually chosen and carried out by children in a small rural school are given.

1 Any subject immediately connected with the child's environment such as: Wild life in my garden/My pets/Local wild flowers/Dogs/Cats/Our family/Life on our farm.
2 A subject based on local historical or geographical background such as: Our school/Our village/History of our manor house/My church/Bark and brass rubbings.
3 Scientifically based subjects such as: Cars/Railways/Aeroplanes/Story of communications.
4 Subjects undertaken in order to organize or acquire knowledge such as: How to look after dogs/Birds of Britain/Sea life and things found on the shore/Parliament and law/Other people's houses/Famous ballerinas/Scouting/Life in different lands/Dancing/Air routes of the world/Australia/First aid.
5 Subjects of current news value which are liable to continue for a few weeks, such as: A royal visit/Death of Sir Winston Churchill/Space flights/Modern music/The FA Cup/Test matches.

To this list can be added any subject given by the various organizations who sponsor competitions connected with this type of work. Such competitions are often of value as a spur to greater effort when interest wanes or as starting points from which to launch off into individual topic work. One other type of topic found to be of considerable interest is the holiday topic in which the child records details of his holiday. Such a topic should demand a minimum of writing and a maximum effort in presentation. It should encourage the collection of everything from picture postcards and brochures of places visited to bus or car parking tickets. These topics can be most attractive and are of considerable interest to the children if kept by them from year to year. They are also a very useful activity for filling in spare time on a wet holiday.

The end product

When we consider the amount of interest and hard work the children put into their individual topic books it is obvious that something positive has to be done with the end product. The children must also be made aware from the start that their efforts are not going to be wasted. This purpose is served by the class topic library, which should be as carefully housed and supervised as all the other school library books available. From past experience it has been found that the keeping of such a library is simplified if all the books are of a standard size. The ordinary school exercise book, quarto size if possible, with an additional cover of stiff cartridge paper is quite suitable.

Once the individual topic library has grown to fifty or so completed books the teacher will find that it becomes a useful source of information for succeeding topics. It is also useful because it will contain both good and bad examples of topic work, and gives the children a chance to compare their own efforts with those of previous and different classes.

The library also encourages children to widen the scope of their choice of subject matter by example or by the mere fact that because a subject has already been well done there is little point in doing another topic on the same subject.

If a standard size of book is used it is quite possible that one book may contain two or even three subjects when this type of work is first introduced. As the children become more competent it also means that more than one volume can be written about the same subject. In actual fact one ten-year-old girl managed to write four small volumes on child welfare during the course of one year.

Supervision and marking

The fact that some individual topics often take the greater part of a term to complete, presents the teacher with the minor problem of supervision, for if the child is to feel free to progress in its own way, and at its own speed, the amount of supervision should be kept to a minimum. Supervision is perhaps best maintained by the teacher expressing interest from time to time in how the work is progressing, and then giving praise where possible. The collection of all the children's topic books each half term also helps to keep an eye on the lazy ones. The books should be awarded marks for content only and handwriting, spelling and punctuation left to be dealt with on other occasions, although this does not mean that the child's English should be allowed to fall below its normal standard.

Assessment

On the completion of a topic the final work should always be discussed with the child in order that mistakes are realized and fresh encouragement is given before another topic is started. It also adds flavour to this work if the child is allowed to give a short lesson or talk to the class on the subject he has written about. Individual topics are really the final end product of all topic work, but like all other subjects the finished article cannot be obtained until the children have first been led quietly through a series of carefully graded steps.

The completed topic should also show ample evidence that the child has gathered information from many sources of reference and that these have been carefully sifted and compared before being expressed in the child's own words.

Finally it is interesting to note that during the course of this work junior children often study subjects which appeal to them as future careers. Can we introduce the choice of a career by this method?

The 'dos' and 'don'ts' of individual topic work

Once a teacher gains experience with this type of work she will discover that children make some mistakes more frequently than others. To help the children avoid these pitfalls she will be wise if she pastes a copy of the following advice on the fly-leaf of the first few individual topic books the children write.

HOW TO IMPROVE YOUR INDIVIDUAL TOPIC BOOK

1 Always print your title page using one colour only. This page should contain the name of the subject you are studying, your name and your age.

2 When printing titles, or making illustrations, only use colours which contrast with the colour of the paper you are using. For example. Black ink shows up well on white paper, white ink does not.

3 Use ink or pencil for writing all the way through your topic. It spoils a topic's appearance if you chop and change from one to the other.

4 If you are using a school exercise book try to fill it up with only one topic. Two or more topics in one exercise book give the impression that you have been too lazy to find enough information on any of them.

5 Only trace a picture when you are unable to draw it yourself, or find another picture which will do. Also see note 9.

6 Always write down what you have found out in your own words. Sometimes you can cut out and paste the entire printed article in your book. In this case it should not take up more than one page of your book.

7 See that all your illustrations are clear and well labelled.

8 Any photographs used must be given a clear title and an explanation if necessary.

9 Only draw portraits if you can make them look like the person concerned. Remember you can always trace them.

10 Titles and Indexes must be made to stand out clearly.

11 Never write a topic using one source of information. Use as many as possible.

12 Make a distinctive cover for your topic book so that other people will notice it, and pick it up to read.

Part Three | Chapter Nine

A Topic on English

While all topics demand the ability to read accurately and to write concise statements they do not necessarily require a child to use English in any other way. As this is so there must quite naturally be a place for a topic which deliberately sets out to improve all branches of the English language including reading, handwriting, spelling, speech training, poetry, essay writing, note taking and drama. A subject topic of this nature is perhaps the most difficult topic to conceive and organize because the 'main aim' can so easily get lost in the subject matter being used as a vehicle for the English. To show how a subject topic on English can be successfully accomplished with a class of ten-year-old children a description of one such topic is given below.

A SUBJECT TOPIC ON ENGLISH

Aim

To give the children an opportunity to improve all aspects of their use of the English language, by making a tape recording suitable for a forty-minute school broadcast on the Civil War 1642–1649.

Teacher preparation

Some three months prior to this English topic a subject/independent group topic was carried out on the Civil War so that the class obtained a good historical background to the period and was conversant with many sources of information. As it happened the most useful sources of information for the English topic were the group topic folders that the class had produced as the end product of their previous Civil War topic.

This topic was also used as the starting point for making a life-sized model of a roundhead soldier during a series of Art and Craft lessons. The model was constructed from plastic bottles covered with papiermâché and took nearly a term to complete. See photograph facing page 129.

Introduction

Once the model was finished the children were encouraged to speculate on what adventures such a soldier might have had. By pretending to be the model many children were persuaded to give vivid verbal accounts of his exploits. Soon it was an easy and natural step for the teacher to suggest making a tape recording of the model's voice so that he could speak for himself.

The children were very excited by this idea but, having carefully planned the topic, the teacher had no intention of their enthusiasm being misdirected or short lived. She insisted that they first named the model. They christened him Joseph Shiner and during the discussion that followed it was agreed that everyone should first have a chance to revise the historical background of the Civil War before writing their own adventure stories during the following week.

From this point the Introduction stage of the topic developed this sequence:

Reading

Non-Fiction Books—Most of these had been read during the previous subject topic on the Civil War but some were referred to by the children when writing their essays.

Fictional Books—As it was foreseen that the tape recording would consist of fiction with a strong historical content the children were encouraged to read novels about the period. These were obtained from the School Library Service and included:

Simon by Rosemary Sutcliff.
Drummer's Den by F. B. Clark.
The Hunted King by Laurence Meynell.
Rosamund Fane by M. and C. Lee.
Gamble for a Throne by Henry Garnett.

The Trumpet and the Swan by M. Bowen.
Silver Guard, The Grey Adventurer, Trumpets in the West by Geoffrey Trease.
Plain Jane and Plain Mill by Barbara Softly.
The Escape of the King by Jane Lane.
Royal Hunt by D. S. Daniell.
The Sword is King, Drum & Trumpet Sound, Vagabond Treasure by S. Ross.
As well as old favourites like *The Children of the New Forest* and *For the King* by Ronald Welch.

Writing

Note taking

During this reading stage the children were asked to write, in about a hundred words, a brief outline of each book they read. The teacher hoped that this would help the children to see the overall plot of each book. This idea was not very popular or successful but it did result in many children making very good notes on each chapter as they read it.

Essays

At the end of a week it became quite obvious from the children's conversation that they had sufficient knowledge of their subject to write an imaginative essay on one aspect of the soldier's life. Two days before they actually wrote their individual essays the teacher reminded the class that Joseph Shiner must have grown up and died somewhere, and that there was nothing to stop them writing about the adventures he might have had before he was a soldier. Quite a few of the girls in the class immediately decided to write about his childhood.

Poetry

While the above activities were taking place a competition was held to see which pupil could collect the most poems concerned with the period, but this proved difficult. Its failure may have been due to the fact that the teacher did not provide the books required. Similarly the children made some attempts at making up poems about Joseph, but for some reason the subject seemed difficult and they were not very good. Again the teacher did not plan this activity well because she wished to push on to the group work while the children's enthusiasm was still high.

Spelling

While praising the content of their work the teacher was particularly hard on any bad spelling she found in the imaginative essays written by the children. She felt this was a very important point as she wished the final written work to be read with some feeling. This, she argued, could not be done if the work was badly misspelt.

Organization of subject

When the individual essays were completed the children obtained a great deal of enjoyment from reading them aloud. This was good practice for reading and quickly made the children realize that the subject gave wide scope for a joint attempt to write Joseph's complete life story. Immediately the idea was mentioned it was discussed. It did not take long for them to draft a rough outline of Joseph Shiner's life and the following plan was drawn up on the blackboard for all to see.

a Joseph's early life from his birth to his leaving home.
b Joseph in training with Cromwell's army.
c Joseph's first battle.
d Joseph's last adventure and death.

Four large independent topic groups were now formed to undertake the task of writing group essays using as much direct speech as possible.

Group essays

While each group confined itself to one part of Joseph's life they took into careful consideration the suggestions made by the other groups while the plan was being drawn up on the blackboard. Everyone pooled ideas for these group essays and by discussion slowly evolved a detailed plot which was in most cases based on the individual essays they had written earlier. With this topic there was very little specific organization within each group. It was noticeable however that while one member wrote out the rough script from the notes they had made during their discussion, others helped by dictating suitable passages from their own individual essays, looked up difficult spellings, corrected doubtful grammar, and arranged suitable sound effects. In another topic of this type a more rigid group organization was used and the subject breakdown can be seen on page 187.

Handwriting

The standard of work produced by the combined efforts of each group was quite good, and after correction by the teacher, each member made a well written copy of their joint essay so that adequate copies were available for the next stage of the topic. See extract on page 186.

These copies were made after the group had carried out a trial run by reading their scripts aloud in the school hall to see if it was easy to follow by ear alone. As a result of this activity, all the groups decided to mention each character's name more frequently when using direct speech. It was also brought home to the children that there was a great need for clear clean handwriting that everyone could read quickly.

Children's Research

There was almost no basic research based on books required for this topic as the children had already carried out this process in their previous topic three months before. Once the tape recorder was used problems did arise.

The need for good breathing and clear speech patterns soon made itself felt and took a few days to achieve.

The teacher took an active part in all rehearsals of the script so that each group could learn by example how to get greater clarity and expression into their reading. The introduction of the tape recorder at this stage was a great help as it allowed recordings to be played back to illustrate common mistakes in speech.

Class Drama

As this topic emphasized the need for clear speech, rather than acting, it took the following pattern:

a Trial recordings made for each piece of group work.

b Further improvement of scripts as the result of class discussions, and listening to the children's recordings.

c The addition of musical interludes to illustrate the passing of time between each group production.
d The election of two children to read Joseph Shiner's part throughout the entire script, i.e. as a boy and as a man.
e Trial recording of the complete production including crowd, camp, battle scenes and marching sound effects.
f The final recording of the topic.

The end product

Because the teacher had recorded the topic one scene at a time her class was naturally very keen to hear the complete recording when it was finished. With the help of the headmaster she assembled the entire school, and with the model of Joseph Shiner standing in the middle of the children she let them listen to the complete recording.

This little bit of stage management had two effects, first it gave her class pride in their achievement, and secondly it proved to be a source of inspiration for a similar topic the following year. The children obtained further pleasure from this topic as their parents heard it relayed when the model of Joseph was displayed at the school's Open Day.

Conclusion

The end product of this topic was not a complete success however, because the final version contained only fifty per cent direct speech and poor sound effects. The following year the same teacher tried a similar topic with another class of ten-year-olds using a model of a Quaker girl as her storyteller. The greater success of this second topic was probably due to better organization of the groups, the use of direct speech for ninety-five per cent of the script and the fact that the entire class arranged the sound effects once the final scripts were ready for recording. See page 187 for an outline plan of this Quaker girl topic.

Both these topics did succeed in giving the children some very practical reasons for improving their standard of reading, writing, spelling, essay work and speech, with the result that there was an all round improvement in their English in other subjects. Thus the topic's 'aim' was achieved.

Part Three | Chapter Ten

Topics and the Student Teacher

Let us first accept the fact that there are many quite simple reasons why the topic method of teaching is one where the student teacher should not expect an instant and resounding success.

For instance, topics demand that the children are left free to move about while using their talents and energies in pursuit of the specific knowledge they are studying. It takes time to create this atmosphere of self-discipline within a classroom, especially if the children are not accustomed to topic work, and the student may therefore find it difficult to achieve this during the few weeks allocated to a school teaching practice.

Furthermore this habit of self-discipline while in the pursuit of knowledge, is normally built up among the children as a result of their experience over a series of topics, so the student should not feel discouraged if it does not happen the first time.

On the other hand nearly all topics will require the student to learn rapidly how to impart, quickly and clearly, quite complicated information to a single child, while at the same time keeping the main stream of work flowing smoothly. Similarly the good student will soon realize that although a subject topic often requires excellent illustrations, its main purpose is to undertake a study of a particular subject or learn a new technique, and that the function of illustrations, models, etc, is to clarify some particular aspect which it would be difficult to present in any other way.

It is agreed that some children find it easier to express their ideas in pictorial form, but here lies the danger that a child's entire interest in the work may be confined to how the illustra-

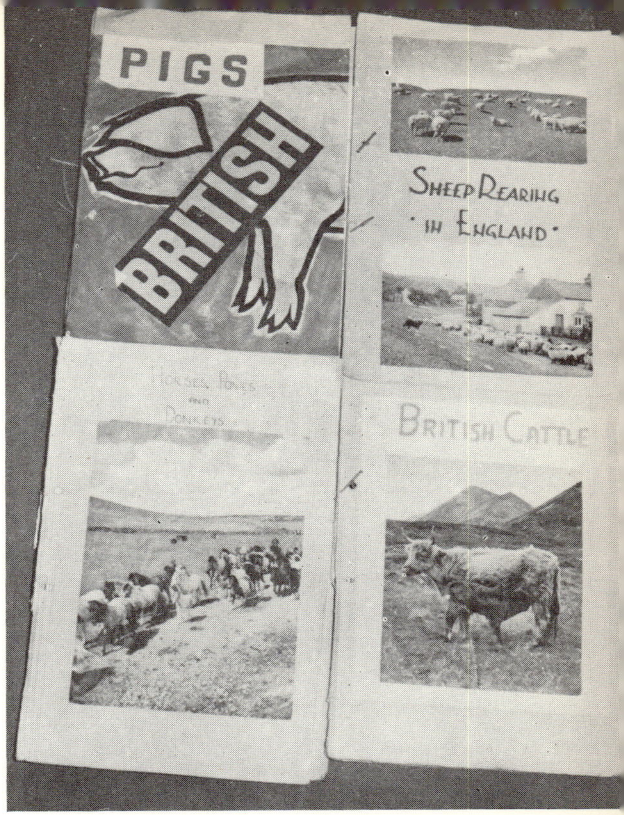

After correspondence with a number of firms during a topic on farm animals, spare advertising material was used to produce these attractive covers for the folders.

Five large wall folders produced by independent groups undertaking a topic on Great Britain.

The topic on Australia shown here was the result of correspondence with a school and the children's relatives in Australia. Most of the information required for this topic was obtained without the use of school textbooks.

tion is made, and not include the subject matter being studied. If this happens the student may find that the children's natural delight in making drawings slowly usurps the proper function of the topic lesson, and converts it into an art and craft lesson.

This realistic appraisal of some of the difficulties of topic work should not deter a student however, for topics are usually exhilarating affairs and there are few problems that a quick read through this chapter will not solve. For even more detailed help on any specific problem the student should turn to the appropriate chapter of this book.

The background assumed for this topic

1 The work is being carried out by a second-year student.
2 The planning starts three weeks before the teaching practice commences.
3 The school is a single entry junior school with four classes.
4 Very little topic work has been carried out by the school.
5 The children are aged 8+ years, have a wide range of ability and are 35 to a class.
6 The school is reasonably well equipped and has built up class libraries of about 300 books mainly connected with history and geography.

The student visits the school

Information required by the student in the order of its importance

1 The student must go to visit the school with a particular topic in mind. An education tutor should have been consulted on this matter beforehand.
2 The headteacher, and class teacher should be informed of the topic and their advice on the subject matter carefully noted. They may make suggestions as to how the topic can be carried out, bearing in mind the problems of their particular school.
3 Next the class teacher should be encouraged to help plan the outline of the topic bearing in mind the facilities, books, etc, she knows are available. At the same time the student should make a copy of the class timetable, and agree with the teacher the amount of time to be spent on topic work.

4 A careful note must be taken about these aspects of the class:
   a The name and age of each child.
   b The local background of the children.
   c The name and type of book the children are reading. Ask the class teacher to point out the best and the worst readers. She may even have a list of reading ages. Ask if it can be copied.
   d Check the type of handwriting being used in the school, i.e. Italic, Marion Richardson, or Cursive. Notice the type of printing the teacher uses for notices, and use the same.
   e Try to get a rough estimate by time and quantity of the amount of writing the children do in their Daily Diary or essay work, so that the written work for the topic can be planned accordingly.
   f Note the names of any children with artistic ability.
   g Try to spot the potential troublemakers in the class and note how the teacher handles them. Think how else they can be dealt with, and write it down.

5 A list of equipment available in the school should be made and the procedure for obtaining it when required should be found out. The school works to a system so the student should be careful not to plan to use the tape recorder etc at the same time as it is required by a permanent member of staff.

6 The class teacher or headteacher should be consulted to ensure that the cardboard, paper, ink, paints, etc, required can be obtained for the topic.

7 Before leaving the school the student should make a note of any school events such as Sports Day which might affect the time available for the topic.

8 The student should try to obtain and sign for, any school textbook which might be helpful when planning the topic, and should take down the details of any suitable films, or filmstrips the school may have.

The initial preparation by the student

 In the three weeks prior to the start of the teaching practice a certain amount of preparation must be carried out and this can be divided into two parts: sources of information and initial outline organization of the topic.

For possible sources of information the student should check the college library and local County Library, for any books connected with the topic subject which the children will be able to read, or from which they can obtain good illustrations. These books must be read to obtain a comprehensive grasp of the subject, because without this it will not be possible to allocate suitable portions of the subject to the various groups of children for study. Suitable material should be sought from the college film and filmstrip library. Any large firm connected with the subject matter of the topic should be asked for any advertisements or educational literature they may have. *The Treasure Chest for Teachers*, published by the Schoolmaster Press, gives a long list of such firms. Any relevant newspaper cuttings, postcards, guide books or maps should be collected.

In preparing the initial organization of the topic the student should write down on a half page of quarto the exact limits of the subject matter to be taught, putting in as many minor subheadings as possible and then try to see how the subject can be split up into five or six parts so that each part will give adequate scope for study by a group of children. (See page 126 for more details on this point.) The next stage is to allocate by name one good reader, and one child of artistic ability to each group. This will at least give a nucleus of organization upon which to build each group later. Finally an approximate time-table of expected progress should be roughed out along the following lines:

First the time available must be calculated.
3 hours per week for 4 weeks = 12 hours of topic time available, plus 3 lessons of Art and Craft if required for illustrations. Then a rough outline of the intended use of each hour should be prepared.

Hour 1 Introduction of topic subject to the class.

2 Further discussion of ideas for studying the subject, allocation of children to groups. Group working areas agreed. The shape of the topic's end product discussed and agreed with the children.

3, 4 & 5	Research by groups. Rough notes taken, letters written, more source material collected.
6	Film or filmstrip shown.
7 & 8	Rough notes written in final form and corrected.
9 & 10	Final notes copied up in good handwriting for topic's end product.
9, 10 & 11	Illustrations drawn or prepared as children finish their written work.
11 & 12	End product of topic prepared and put together. Study and discussion of results by the class.

Topics never quite go according to plan, but they go much better if there is a plan.

Details of a topic carried out by a student under conditions described above

Topic subject: A bar of fruit and nut chocolate.
Type of topic: Subject/independent groups.
Class: 35 children aged 8+ years.
Time taken: About 15 hours + Art and Craft lessons of 3 hours.

All topics require considerable preparation and planning, and to facilitate this most class topics can be fitted into the basic framework of Teacher Preparation; Introduction; Organization of Subject; Children's Research; End Product. To this list can be added an 'aim' so that right from the beginning the student has a clear-cut image of what she is trying to achieve.

The 'aims' of the topic

Each topic should have a clear aim stated in a few words. Normally the 'aim' can be obtained by checking the school's syllabus of work at the beginning of each term to see which items can become the basis for a topic. Sometimes a topic can have two 'aims', in which case one is the main aim and the other the subsidiary aim.

With subject topics the main aim will state the subject matter being studied, and the subsidiary aim will state what techniques of topic work are to be revised. For this topic the student decided on the following aims:

Main Aim: To show how different nations contribute their produce to make a bar of fruit and nut chocolate.
Subsidiary Aim: To revise the idea of each group working on a separate aspect of the main subject, i.e. independent topic groups.

Teacher preparation

The student did a considerable amount of work to ensure that the children had an adequate supply of information on the subject of the topic. She visited libraries, obtained copies of film-strips, obtained help from the school's headmaster and wrote to a large number of firms for literature.

Introduction

With the bar of fruit and nut chocolate topic it was decided to introduce the subject in the form of an essay lesson which was well prepared by the student. First large bars of chocolate were shown to the class and a discussion held on their looks, smell, feel and taste. The question of taste was very popular because each child was given a small lump to eat. After about fifteen minutes, the words look, smell, feel, sound and taste were written on the blackboard along with a number of descriptive words suggested by the class. The subsequent essays on 'A Bar of Chocolate' not only introduced the topic subject but also gave the student a very good measure of each child's ability. She was able to complete her allocation of children to topic groups bearing these facts in mind. At the end of the essay lesson the children were asked to collect the wrapping papers from as many chocolates and cocoa products as possible. This was turned into a competition and a small bar of chocolate offered for the best collection made before the next topic lesson.

Organization of subject

Prior to the research stage of a topic an outline plan is required showing how the subject matter can be divided up into fairly equal portions so that each group of children have adequate scope for their researches into the information available. (See Chapter Fourteen.) To this must be added the number and type of children most suitable for the work involved. As the children and the student were new to topic work she made no attempt to get the children to choose their own section of the topic work. She simply allocated the children she considered would be most suitable for each group. This selection was based on the knowledge she obtained from the class teacher and her own observations of their essay work. Before the second topic lesson the student divided the subject into group assignments on: Cocoa beans and nuts/Milk/Sugar cane/Sugar beet/Dried fruits/Citrus fruits/Paper. To each of these sections she allocated a group of children selected by ability in order that each group should have an equal amount of talent. Once the group work was allocated the student helped each group to sort out their subject so that every child had his fair share of the work.

Research stage

Each group of children confined their researches to the subject they had been allocated, with the result that the group booklets contained the following information:

Cocoa Beans and Nuts Group

Where cocoa grows—Ghana, Brazil, Nigeria, Cameroon, Equador and Dominican Republic/How cocoa grows/Life in a cocoa village, the cocoa market/Transport—how cocoa is shipped and bagged/History of cocoa, in Africa, in England/Making cocoa and chocolate in England, details of manufacture/Where Brazil, almond and hazel nuts come from/How they are harvested, roasted and added to chocolate.

Milk Group

Lands where cows are found and farmed/The cow—feeding, calves, vets, prices, sale of cows/The various types of cow found in Britain/Milk—the details of how it gets from the dairy to the chocolate factory/How milk is added to chocolate.

Sugar Cane Group

Where sugar cane grows and how we import it/The history of sugar growing/How sugar cane grows/How it is turned into sugar at the factory/How and why it is added to chocolate.

Sugar Beet Group

Where sugar beet is grown in the world/The history of sugar beet/Where it is grown in England/How it grows and the conditions required for good growth/Harvesting the crop and the machines used/How it is treated at the factory/The by-products obtained from sugar beet.

Citrus Fruits Group

World map showing the location of citrus fruits growing/ Drawing of various types of fruit/Map showing the wholesale fruit markets in Britain/The growth, transport and sale of oranges/The growth, transport and sale of limes, lemons and grapefruit.

Dried Fruits Group

Drawings of all the dried fruits available/Details of how they were all grown/How grapes are grown and details of wine making/Description of how fruits are dried and why/Various uses of dried fruits/How and when they are added to chocolate.

Paper Group

Why chocolate is wrapped in paper—hygiene, storage, advertisement/How paper helps in storage and transportation/ Various methods used to wrap products of cocoa—paper bags, wrapping paper, boxes, cartons/The various shapes packed, cocoa tins, boxes of chocolates, Easter eggs/How paper is made/ Where woodpulp comes from/How paper is printed/Cost of wrapping paper, and the machines that wrap cocoa.

Because the student was inexperienced at this work she tended to impose the above outline plan on the class because she had prepared it with some care prior to her teaching practice. Probably she was right to do so, but with a little experience she could have obtained an equally suitable plan from the children by spending a little longer on the discussion stage of the work.

After a few topic lessons when the children had settled down to the work the student felt they would benefit from a filmstrip lesson on cocoa. This proved of great use, since it reminded them of the central theme of the topic and gave them a chance to discuss and organize the considerable amount of knowledge they had already obtained.

The end product

When the written work and illustrations were finished each group made a folder cover for their work. These folders (10 by 12 inches) were made from manilla paper with a different colour for each group. The outsides were decorated with advertising material illustrating the contents. The internal sheets consisted of coloured kitchen paper on to which the children's work had been glued. These folders were hung on the classroom wall and then surrounded by a large display of wall charts, booklets, and other display material that had been obtained from the various manufacturers during the course of the topic.

Conclusion

Considering that the children had never carried out a topic before, they learnt a considerable amount about their subject and produced a very good end product. During the time allowed for a discussion to assess the qualities of their work, the children expressed their own satisfaction with the results.

The student obtained an enlightening insight into the problems of topic work, particularly the need for adequate preparation. In fact, due to the pressure of work at college, the student was unable to undertake an extensive course of reading prior to carrying out the topic on teaching practice. Without such reading any topic work is liable to failure. In this case however she obtained some extremely informative booklets from four firms she had written to during the planning stage and these proved adequate preparation for her needs.

Part Three | Chapter Eleven

The Headteacher and Topic Work

Problems of establishing topic work in a school

One of the tasks of every headteacher is to keep abreast of new trends in education and to evaluate their usefulness in his school. It is also his task to persuade members of his staff to take an interest in new ideas, and if possible, arrange for a certain amount of experimental work to be carried out in the classroom. Most headteachers will, I believe, agree that new methods should be introduced slowly into a school, and in their early stages, never be allowed to conflict with the established pattern of the school.

Because they always have the welfare of their children at heart, and because they are vitally aware that they may adversely affect the future progress of the children, teachers do not readily accept a change in the teaching methods they have found successful in the past. Fortunately, the best approach to the establishment of topic work within a school is to introduce the method slowly over a number of years, because topics should never be regarded as embracing all the answers to our teaching problems. It will be a much more realistic approach, if headteachers regard topic work as an exciting and stimulating tool to be used with, and alongside, other known and successful ways of educating children.

Staffing and continuity

Sometimes staffing problems loom large on the horizon of a headteacher and to start on a new idea appears most difficult, especially if a lack of continuity in staff looks like breaking up a long term project before it has really had time to establish itself.

Topic work should never be considered in this light as its success, or failure, lies mainly in the children receiving the appropriate level of instruction in the method year by year. As with the teaching of mathematics and reading, a graded scheme of work can be devised so that every teacher in the school is responsible for teaching a limited number of techniques. The required standard of work can therefore be achieved at the top of the junior school despite a few changes in the teaching staff.

In the past teachers have too often attempted to obtain the final advantages of topic work without laying down a firm foundation for such work over a number of years. It is important therefore that headteachers accept the principle that, like all other new subjects introduced into the curriculum, time is an important factor in introducing the techniques and skills involved.

The headteacher's task

As with all classroom subjects, the headteacher's attitude plays an important part in helping his staff to create the right atmosphere in which to achieve success, and as topics require careful preparation, headteachers will find that they have a vital part in nearly all the topics carried out in their school.

The organization of a school is the responsibility of a headteacher and the following questions are some of those with which he can expect to be faced when wishing to introduce topics into his school. A possible approach to each problem has been given after each question.

Where in the junior school can topic work best be introduced?

If a school has never attempted this type of work before it is advisable to introduce it into the lowest junior form first. Then as this form progresses through the school, the teaching staff will have a chance of studying the effect the introduction of the various grades of topic have upon the children's work. This will also allow each teacher in turn to build upon the experiences and techniques taught by previous teachers as the class grows older. Headteachers must encourage staff teamwork with topic teaching so that both successful and unsuccessful ideas are discussed and recorded for future reference.

Where a school has already established a system of topic work, there is no reason why the knowledge gained should not be weighed against the contents of this book. It may well reveal that a little more careful grading of the work will be an added advantage.

Where, in our crowded timetables, can this type of work be fitted?

In most primary schools, history and geography are already combined into an outline scheme of work covering a period of four years. There are also a large number of class textbooks produced by many publishers which supplement each other in their approach to the study of these subjects. This being so, headteachers will find it reasonably easy to carry out a number of topics in these subjects without disturbing the established pattern of the school.

Time is required for a topic, and it is suggested that each period should last about $1\frac{1}{4}$ hours. A minimum of two periods a week are required if the children's interest in the work is not to wane. These large blocks of time appear difficult to organize until it is realized that topic work embraces all aspects of the use of English including reading, comprehension, language study, dictionary and reference work, handwriting, spelling and essay writing on a given theme. If headteachers, when drawing up their yearly timetables, arrange for every geography and history period to be followed by an English period, the two periods can be lumped together for topic work when required. In those schools were an integral day operates, and where topic work is already established, its enlargement should present few problems.

Which kind of teacher should undertake topic work?

Any teacher worthy of that title should enjoy topic work. It is pointed out however that only people capable of evoking self-discipline from the children will ever be highly successful at the work.

How is topic work connected with the more formal work carried out in other lessons during the rest of the term?

A topic should not be regarded as an isolated piece of work but should be built up from subject matter within the school's existing scheme of work. It should continue the natural sequence and flow of the subject under study and by introducing a new method of learning, it should allow a more detailed study of one particular part of a subject. For example, when a term is allocated to a general study of the British Isles a topic may be carried out into the details of coal mining in Britain, as a part of that general study. Topics must call for more individual effort on the part of every child to seek facts in new ways, and present them in the most attractive form possible.

If a headteacher replaces the old type of exercise book for say history and geography with a hard covered, spring clip type folder (suitable for quarto-sized paper), it will be found that, not only will these folders hold up to two years' work for both subjects, but that the supply of paper is cheaper than the supply of exercise books. Further, it should be noted that any illustrations, or map work duplicated for use by the children can be quite easily fitted into the folder at the right place.

Ring binders covered in PVC coated paper (washable) are available in a number of colours and those that hold a sheet size 10 by 8 inches are the most suitable kind of folder. When a topic is carried out rough notes, unused illustrations, etc, can be placed in the folder so that it becomes quite evident where the topic came within the pattern of the year's work.

What other materials, or facilities does the teacher of topics require?

In all topic work there should be some form of end product, and at each stage the age and ability of the children will help to determine what form it will take. It is usually best in the early stages, to let the end product be something which can be displayed in such a way that every child's work is easily visible. This provides a real incentive for every child to give of his best, not only on the first occasion, but on all subsequent occasions. The headteacher must therefore be prepared to provide the material teachers will require to display the children's work to advantage. Among other things this will mean providing various sizes of mounting paper such as:

a Kitchen paper in various colours. 30 by 20 ins is a good size.

b Rolls of exhausted dyline paper. 50 yds by 30 ins.

c Coloured cardboard of 6-sheet thickness. 20 by 25 ins is a useful size.
d Square cut file covers, buff manilla without clips in foolscap size.

Various writing and printing materials will be required such as:

a Ball-point pens of various colours.
b Felt markers of various colours.
c Wax pencils and crayons.
d Coloured Indian inks.
e Poster paints.

Methods of holding paper together are required such as:

a Clear adhesive tape, roll sizes ½ in to 1 in.
b Treasury tags ½ in to 1 in.
c Wallpaper paste, preferably cellulose.
d Two-hole punches, adjustable 7 cm to 8 cm.
e Stapling machines. The long arm type is most useful.
f Leather punch, multi-size hole type with rotating head. Available from Dryads, Leicester.

Other facilities required by teaching staff:

a Use of school duplicator, with a good supply of paper, etc.
b Use of school typewriter, or the services of the school secretary, for the production of duplicated booklets, question cards, information sheets, etc.
c Use of the school's system for being supplied with library books from the LEA Library Service so that teachers can order their requirements for topic work some weeks in advance.
d Teachers should have access to the publishers' catalogues which come with nearly every post. These often indicate new and attractively presented books on subjects suitable for study by topic methods. They also help to keep the teachers up to date with new techniques of teaching which can be included in their next class topic.
e Each teacher can be allocated a small sum of money with which they can purchase books particularly suitable for topic work in their own class.

f If each classroom is only supplied with a selection of textbooks for, say, nature study, history, or geography, it helps teachers if they have a copy of each book in the series available in the school. Each teacher must be made aware of what has come before, and what is yet to come, in any scheme of work and should never be asked to work without reference to her colleagues' work.

g The posting facilities of the school should be available so that both the teachers and the children can write away for additional information on a subject. Once a child has had the thrill of receiving a letter at school, letter writing soon becomes an enjoyable occupation as well as a good source of useful material for both child and teacher.

h Teachers should be encouraged to send for and inspect suitable filmstrips, or to borrow them from the various sources available. The problems involved in the use of the school projector should be reconsidered and reduced to the minimum because time is important.

i The school tape recorder should be freely available. If each teacher is made responsible for some tapes which belong to her own classroom alone, then problems of record keeping and recording are solved.

In what way can headteachers encourage their staffs to take an interest in topic work?

Surely one of the best solutions to this problem is for headteachers to set an example by undertaking a topic, probably with an assistant teacher's help. This will also enable a headteacher to assess from personal experience the best ways of adapting the method to his own school and the school's environment.

Visits by teachers to other schools where topic work is well established is another, but less rewarding method of assessing the problems involved. By close cooperation with other schools however, and the pooling of knowledge and experience gained, each school can benefit from the efforts of others. If treated in this way topic work can reduce needless rivalry between schools and replace it with an honest desire on the part of the teachers to gain fresh knowledge on new techniques of learning.

In what other ways can a headteacher assist his staff with this work? Headteachers will assist their staff by locating, and organizing as many places, people, and organizations of interest outside school which might make suitable starting points for a topic. A head who has personal contacts in the Fire Service, Police Station, Hospital, Bus Station, local factories and farms, or knowledge of local places of interest, will be in a good position to give constructive help to the younger members of his staff.
How can topics be organized in a large urban school where classes are streamed by ability and age?
Obviously a topic can be carried out with any type of class in any type of school, but it can also be used to loosen up a school's internal organization when it has become too rigid.

In such schools the 'block system' can be adopted for topic work, and one of the most suitable units for this form of organization is four classes of similar age but widely differing ability. The teachers normally responsible for these classes should act as a joint planning team for the topic. This is helped if one of the four teachers accepts the role of coordinator, and one lesson period per week is set aside for a teacher's co-ordinating session. The four original classes should be re-organized into four new classes each containing a complete cross section of the children available. In many schools this can be quickly achieved by having all the children of one particular 'House' or 'Team' in one topic class. Thus if there happens to be four team colours in the school, four fairly representative classes are quickly formed. If three blocks of time of about two hours each are allocated per week, the topic should proceed smoothly provided that all the teachers accept the responsibility for improving the overall standard of the children's English and divide the subject between them so that each is responsible for teaching one particular aspect of it to all four classes in turn. The teachers should also share the task of seeking suitable books, filmstrips, places to visit, etc., as this is all part of team teaching.

Conclusion

Finally, the headteacher should keep a detailed record of all topics carried out in his school over a period of years so that the children's and teachers' interests can be catered for when ordering books and materials. Perhaps the best way of keeping this record is to store the completed topics themselves.

From time to time it is not a bad thing to display topics which are five or more years old in order that everyone can see what ideas have been improved upon, or used previously and then forgotten.

Such topics often form a pool of local knowledge from which members of staff can seek ideas, or into which they can, on occasions, be pushed!

Part Three | Chapter Twelve

Books and Topic Work

Reasons for reading

If we are to persuade children to use books we must not only teach them to read, but also give them a reason for reading, and what better reason can they have than the desire to obtain more information about some active and enjoyable physical experience they have undergone?

This process of contact with the physical world in order to generate the desire for knowledge, is, in the early stages of topic work, an essential prerequisite to the children's contact with books.

The supply of books

Unfortunately the supply of an adequate number of suitably graded books for topic work is still too often the teacher's major problem when starting a topic. In many cases this difficulty can be overcome by recourse to the County Library Service for schools. The quality of this service varies from county to county, but it should be large enough, and frequent enough, to supply a teacher with at least half the books she requires to run a topic on some relatively well-known subject, such as wild flowers or coal mining.

It has always been my experience that if the librarians are given a few weeks' notice of a teacher's requirements, they are not only tolerant of our idiosyncrasies, but are also extremely helpful in suggesting the appropriate books.

The school library

Most primary schools are still unable to allocate a separate room for use as a library, but this is no excuse for preventing the children from having a free access to all the books which are available. Where the supply of books is adequate this problem can be overcome by having class libraries and a small central reference library. The main object should always be to display the books attractively so that the children can select and change their books at will, and not be restricted to short periods of time throughout the week.

Where there is space in the classroom for their display and use there are many advantages in having the books there for quick reference.

Books in the classroom

While the books in a classroom may, from lack of space, have to remain at a static figure, it is essential that there is a constant inward and outward flow of books so that the children's interest is constantly aroused by being challenged by the contents of new books.

Organization of classroom books

In a junior school, whether books are held in a library, or in the classroom they should be divided into four types: subject information books; fiction; reference; and graded textbooks.

Subject books

Junior school books dealing with specific subjects are best grouped under subject headings, rather than by authors, as this reduces the problems involved when children are seeking information.

Fiction books

Books of fiction should be placed under authors in a different location in the classroom, or library. This helps, in the early years, to highlight the point that, while certain books are written in such a style that they appear to deal with historical or scientific facts, they are, in reality, only the lively imagination of an author's mind. It also enables a child who likes a particular author to read all his works over a period of time. Children soon learn to look for the author's name when seeking a suitable reading book from the local library or mobile van.

Reference books

These should be placed where they are easily accessible to everyone.

Graded textbooks

There are many advantages in keeping these in a separate section of the library which is clearly marked with the type of book it contains.

Assessing new books

To be really competent at topic work the teacher should have a wide knowledge of the books available within her classroom, and an ability to remember likely sources of information on any subject which is due for discussion. To do this the teacher must read and digest, the majority of the books under her control. If she does this, she will radiate such confidence among books that the children will long to follow her example, for there is nothing so contagious as success. By reading the children's books she will also be in a good position to assess the quality of the books available and to discuss their good and bad features with the children.

The qualities required of a topic book

It is impossible in a book of this type to deal fully with the subject of school books, but the following points should be borne in mind when choosing topic books for juniors:

1 The type of book which gives detailed references, through page numbers, is better than one which only provides a list of chapter headings.
2 The size and clarity of printing type used is important if the book is to be used by young children who are poor readers.
3 The actual size and weight of a book should be taken into account. In this respect junior children seem to prefer quarto-sized books with clear and colourful illustrations.

4 Children often notice the quality of the paper used, and prefer good paper because it allows clear drawings and photographs.
5 The sequence in which the subject matter is presented to children is not always easy to follow in some books and they find ones with bold subheadings easier to work with in topics.

Books used for topic work

Books are the main rock upon which the majority of topics are built and some types of book are obviously more useful than others.

One cannot dogmatically state the function of the various types of book available, but over the course of many topics the following observations can be made.

Encyclopedias are invaluable as a means of obtaining a quick outline of a subject and are therefore an excellent starting point from which an investigation of a subject can take place. Pictorial reference books can reinforce knowledge already obtained from the more formal type of encyclopedia by giving the children good visual images of the subject under study.

Sets of four, or more, graded textbooks are available on a wide range of school subjects, and these have been found most useful as sources of information. They are particularly useful because they provide the children with a wide variety of facts which are presented to them in words and phrases designed to suit their reading ages. A small class library containing three or four copies, of all the current textbooks available on a subject, irrespective of publisher, is an extremely valuable aid to topic work.

Subject books

These are books, often published in series, which confine their information to a single subject. Most of the series in this type of book are designed to appeal to upper juniors and above, but lower juniors for some reason find them attractive and a useful source of pictorial information.

Books of fiction, particularly historical fiction, provide an attractive and easily read background to life in other countries, or periods in recorded history. The County Librarian should be consulted for titles suitable for background reading on any particular subject as they often have this type of information in their library files.

Children find the simple general knowledge book such as *The sea around us* by Rachel Carson and *Looking at Nature* by Elsie Proctor, very enjoyable reading, and frequently this type of book becomes the starting point for many individual topics with the upper juniors.

How to keep track of new books

New publications are not difficult to trace provided the teacher has time to spare. Spare time however is one thing a good teacher rarely has and it is suggested that this problem is approached by taking a note of suitable books mentioned in the book reviews of the better class of Sunday and daily newspapers and educational papers and magazines, by referring to publishers' catalogues which frequently make a point of highlighting new publications, and by obtaining from time to time the duplicated lists of new books which most County Libraries provide free of charge.

The teacher should be constantly alert to spot any new trends in publications, for publishers are always trying to produce the type of books which the more progressive type of teacher requires.

Out of date reference books

Many organizations and associations publish a yearly reference book, e.g. the AA Handbook, Telephone Directories.

Most County Libraries throw a large number of this type of book away each year, and many can be used for topic work. For example one school obtained thirty very interesting reference books this way including *Frozen Foods Yearbook*; *National Trust Properties*; *Annual Charities Digest*; *The Fruit Annual*; *Interavia ABC Directory of Aviation.*

The problem of selecting books

Frequently the time allowed for the selection of suitable books is completely inadequate and both teachers and children are forced to make a hasty choice from the books available from a library. This is sometimes the fault of the school timetable and sometimes it is due to the fact that the mobile schools' library van is due at another school at a fixed time. The subsequent problems which arise from such hasty proceedings can be partly solved by building up a large and detailed reference section in the school, or class library.

It is also advisable to keep a record of the type of books which would have been useful during a topic and send a list to the School Library Service a few days before they are next due at the school. This does not solve a problem but it prevents it occurring again in future.

American books

Some American books of good quality are finding their way into our schools, but care must be taken to point out the differences in spelling which occur. To set the children some simple game concerned with finding these words as they read the book is perhaps the easiest way of drawing attention to this problem.

Historical documents

The well produced collections of reproductions of contemporary documents published by Jackdaw Publications Ltd are a cheap and informative service of information for many historical topics.

When no County Library Service for schools exists

Where a library service does not exist, or is inadequate, the teacher must find other and less suitable means of supplying printed material for her class. In this respect, the realm of advertising can supply a wealth of brightly illustrated booklets containing detailed information on many subjects. Many large firms do in fact welcome requests from teachers, and go to considerable lengths to produce pamphlets geared to project and topic work.

Part Three | Chapter Thirteen

Information — Its Sources, Collection and Organization

All topic work should actively encourage children to seek the knowledge available on a subject from a wide variety of sources before they undertake the task of correlating it into a balanced and logically informative piece of English.

In order to do this they will be required to use some of the following sources of information:

The child

The child, or the child's family may have personal knowledge of a trade, locality, or area.

Local people

The local shopkeeper, policeman, garage owner and clergyman can all prove mines of information on local affairs and local history.

Any famous personality living locally may be prepared to talk to school children for a short while, provided they receive adequate notice.

Books

All books found in school, the local library and at home, should be referred to. Newspapers and magazines are extremely useful as sources from which illustrations can be obtained. The subject of books is dealt with more fully in Chapter Twelve.

Radio and television

Sometimes programmes can be used to build up a general background to a topic subject even if they do not actually deal with the subject itself. For example, a television play set in Northern Canada will usually give background views of the country inhabited by Eskimos, and this would be a great help to a child doing a topic on the peoples of Canada.

Filmstrips

While those available may not actually deal with the topic subject being studied by the class, one or two of the frames from a strip on another subject may be useful when illustrations have to be drawn.

Pictures and photographs

Old textbooks, newspapers and magazines are obvious sources, but the local art gallery, local printing firm and personal photographs are also useful.

Art galleries

Most of the national art galleries print cheap coloured postcards of their better known paintings. As many of these paintings are of famous people or events, they provide a colourful addition to most topics. A list of galleries can be obtained from HM Stationery Office, London SE I.

Letters

Many manufacturing firms provide free advertising material concerning their products, and in some cases these take the form of quite elaborate booklets. The children should write a rough draft of the letter for correction by the teacher. Then two good copies should be made. One to be sent by post, the other for inclusion in the topic so that a record of correspondence is kept.

Records and recordings

Gramophone records can provide a background to certain subjects, e.g. music topics. It is also possible to obtain recordings of actual events as they happened. The BBC will sometimes provide them.

Samples and free gifts

 Some firms provide free gifts and wall charts which are appropriate to a topic subject. The British Trades Alphabet (a magazine provided free of charge from Alpha House, East Ardsley, Wakefield, Yorkshire) gives a list of firms supplying suitable material.

Museums — local and national

Museums usually provide an information service, booklets and picture postcards of their exhibits. Some even provide models for use in schools. Members of their staff are sometimes prepared to come and talk to the children.

Stately Homes and Town Halls

Many provide very well illustrated brochures at a very reasonable cost.

Lectures

Short talks by the children themselves can sometimes provide specialized knowledge. For example the policeman's son can often provide refreshingly new knowledge both for the teacher and the rest of the class about the police force.

Other schools and colleges

Many teachers have outside interests which take them into other spheres of life. If this does not apply to your school, try the staff of other local schools. Most headteachers know their local colleagues quite well and can usually make the necessary arrangements.

The telephone

Children should be made aware of its use as a means of obtaining vital information which is urgently required.

Trade magazines

These often contain specialized information which is a little difficult for the junior child to understand, but their advertising pages are an excellent source of illustrations for many topics.

Foreign Embassies in London

Many of these provide considerable quantities of information on their country free of charge. They should be provided with a large stamped addressed envelope to prevent any mistakes in your address when they reply.

The County Archivist

This is an excellent source of information on local affairs and can usually be located via your County Hall. Most County Archivist offices are understaffed and overworked, so have patience when dealing with this source.

Local Newspaper

Newsmen are very busy people and cannot be expected to provide great quantities of information. On the other hand they are experts on where unusual information can be found.

Local Societies

Most localities contain people who between them belong to hundreds of societies. For example your local doctor may be a keen archaeologist or yachtsman. As the address of these societies' local Secretary is frequently quite difficult to find, ask your local newspaper office, or County Archivist if they can help. Failing that write to the Headquarters of the Society. This is usually in London and their telephone number and address can be obtained through the telephone service.

Special books giving sources of information

Whitaker's Almanack provides addresses and sources of information for nearly every subject connected with life in the British Isles. *Facts and How to find them* written by W. A. Bagley is a useful book to have available in the classroom. *Treasure Chest for Teachers* contains names and addresses of societies and associations which have some bearing on the school curriculum. This book should be available in all schools where child-centred teaching is carried out.

Sources and aids to information usually provided by the teacher

Map work

Children should be encouraged to draw their own maps whenever possible and teachers should see that various types of atlas are available in the classroom.

School duplicator

The teacher can provide outline maps and illustrations for completion, or colouring, by the children.

Tracing paper

Some pictures are too difficult to draw, and a tracing can be taken. Tracing has a use, but children should be encouraged to do their own drawings whenever possible.

Poems

Sometimes poems can be composed by the children to describe an aspect of their topic. If the school library contains a good selection of poetry books it is frequently possible to find a suitable poem for inclusion in a topic.

Paintings and lino cuts

Art lessons are very useful for the production of pictures and lino cuts connected with a topic of current interest to the children.

Old people

Many old people are a wonderful source of knowledge. By means of a tape recorder the teacher can bring their eye witness accounts of past events, and their personal stories right into the classroom.

Books as a source of information

The teacher of junior school children will have to give them some guidance on how to use a book correctly when seeking information. Such guidance can be reinforced at about Grade 3 of topic work by giving each child a duplicated sheet similar to the following, which will last longer if duplicated on thin card rather than paper and will also be easier to find among the litter of books and papers on a child's desk during topic work.

HOW TO USE A BOOK WHEN SEEKING INFORMATION

1 Find out the chief characters and facts involved in a subject you wish to write about by first referring to a suitable encyclopedia. This will give you a brief outline picture of your subject.

2 Now widen the scope of your knowledge by first referring to books which have a title dealing with your subject e.g. If you wish to write about the discovery of America, a book with a title such as 'History of America' is very likely to tell you what you wish to know.

3 Having found a suitable book, look up the contents list which is usually in the front of the book, but is sometimes found at the end. Read the summary of contents, and see if there is a chapter on the subject you seek. If there is not, do not waste time looking through the pages of the book - try another book.

4 If you wish to find the exact page on which a particular person, or fact, is mentioned, turn to the index of the book. If there is an index it is usually placed at the back of the book. Now look up the person, or fact, concerned and the index will give you the pages in the book where they are mentioned. If more than one page is given do not be content until you have checked them all.

5 Never use only one or two books as your source of information. Read as many books on your subject as possible and take extremely brief notes as you do so. No more than six lines of notes for every chapter is a reasonable guide.

6 Having completed your researches and obtained a good grasp of your subject you must:

a Organize the information you have obtained in a logical sequence.
b Write it out in your own words, using the short notes you have taken. You will be surprised how much additional information you remember as you start to write.
c Add any suitable maps, pictures, drawings, or diagrams which you have found.

Part Three | Chapter Fourteen

Planning a Topic

Before starting out to study a topic subject the teacher or the child must ascertain that the subject itself provides enough depth to make a detailed study of it worth undertaking.

To do this the subject must be viewed from various directions and an assessment made as to whether the various aspects which appear are worthy of further investigation.

Once satisfied that the suggested subject will provide enough scope, a detailed outline plan similar to those given in Appendix One should be prepared.

The requirements of an outline plan

All class topics in the junior school will necessitate the teacher constructing an outline plan before the class starts work. In the early grades this will be done without help from the class. Later the teacher and children should combine their knowledge to construct the final plan for their topic.

This plan must provide a basis for dividing the class up into working groups and divide the topic subject up in such a way that the amount of work involved in each group assignment is roughly equal. The plan must, however, remain flexible enough to allow for improvement by the children. It must also be simple enough to be easily understood when written on the blackboard and ensure that a comprehensive study of the subject is made by the class. Long outline plans like the example given in Chapter Three may have to be duplicated once they are finalized.

The teacher's personality and the outline plan

How a teacher sets about constructing an outline plan for a topic will depend very largely upon her methods of making a logical plan of action when dealing with any of life's problems. Since this is so what follows is mainly in the form of a suggestion.

Constructing an outline plan

Teachers must realize that no one can construct an adequate outline plan of a subject unless they already possess a reasonable knowledge of the subject, gained from their past studies of it, or can rapidly acquire a knowledge of the subject from books, or some other means such as films, television, museums, etc.

Assuming that the topic subject is one with which the teacher is reasonably familiar she can proceed as follows:

1 To jot down, quite haphazardly, all the aspects of the subject, just as they enter her head.
2 Without attempting to put these notes into a logical sequence she should consider each of these notes in turn and jot down a further list of ideas she associates with them.
3 Having by now compiled a fair sized list of ideas concerning the subject she should group them in a logical order under four or five major headings depending on how many working groups she requires.
4 She should now examine her embryo plan to try and see what she has *omitted* and include any new aspects which occur to her (and the children) as being associated with the groupings she has already made.
5 The final outline plan should be brief and should have well spaced group headings, each with neat notes under them.

This final blackboard plan should be something which can be referred to at a glance without getting lost.

Other ways of constructing an outline plan

The outline plan for some topics can be quickly organized by basing them on a chronological order of events; a production sequence; the life cycle of an animal, or plant; or the seasons of the year.

Using the outline plan

While the teacher's outline plan of a subject may be improved by the children, if it has been well prepared it will become the framework upon which the children will carry out their own detailed investigation, either in groups, or individually.

Later, when the end products of the children's researches are collated, the outline plan can be used to see that a complete coverage of a subject has been achieved.

Outline plans and individual topics

When children reach the upper junior level they should be asked to construct their own outline plans for individual topic work. Many children find this difficult as their knowledge of the world is so limited.

To overcome this difficulty the teacher should encourage the children to construct an outline plan for every individual topic they undertake.

She should help them to do this by asking them to read the following list, and then consider their topic subject:

a Where is it?
b When is it?
c Why is it?
d Who did it?
e What did it?
f How does it taste, feel, smell, hear, see and think?
g What have you learnt about it from your study of: History/Geography/Nature/Art/Scripture/Mathematics/English/Music/Sport?
h Have you read a book about the subject?
i Have you looked it up in an encyclopedia?
j Have you asked your parents and friends about it?

The teacher should then check every outline plan, whether group or individual, before the children start work, and remind them to organize their topic so that it includes an index, chapter headings, a list of sources of information, any correspondence connected with the topic and a short description of how they carried out the work.

The limits of an outline plan

It may be that having constructed an outline plan of a subject the teacher, or child, finds that the topic subject chosen is too wide to be covered by one topic. In this case the subject can either become the basis of a series of topics, or undertaken by only touching lightly on each aspect in turn. This type of subject is very suitable for a Grade 6 topic. For an example of this see the one given at the end of this chapter.

Alternatively an outline plan may reveal that a subject is too restricted in its scope, or not suitable for studying by children of a particular age group, which is probably the reason for the failure of some topics.

Conclusion

It is quite likely that two people, starting with the same subject, and compiling similar lists of aspects of it, may arrive at quite different outline plans.

The fact that all these plans may be equally effective, and valid, is one factor that keeps topic work fresh and a constant challenge to both the teacher and child over many years.

Example showing the construction of an outline plan

Topic subject: Horses.

The first list about horses which occurred to a teacher was: Working horses/Racing/Ponies/Plough/Lord Mayor's coach/ War horses.

This haphazard list was reread and the following aspects added: Structure of horses/Cost of horses/Feeding/Diseases/ Housing/Equipment/Polo ponies/Shows/Jumping horses.

Five groups of six children were required for this particular class topic, so the various aspects were gathered together and others added as follows:

GROUP 1 *Working*	GROUP 2 *History*	GROUP 3 *Equipment*	GROUP 4 *Food and Illness*	GROUP 5 *Housing and Transport*
Farm	War	For horse	Food costs	Types of stable
Racing	Mayor's coach	For trade	Vet's costs	Horse boxes
Hunting	Development of horses	For grooms	Preventing illness	Horse trains, ships and aeroplanes
Pony clubs	Breeding	For rider	Structure of horse	
Shows	Famous horses	For owner	Illnesses due to trades	Cost of show transport
Polo	The Life Guards	Costs		Olympic Games problems

A study of horses is obviously going to be a wide subject with plenty of scope for each child. Other aspects of the subject not yet mentioned are: Dartmoor ponies/Shetland ponies/Donkeys/Mules/Use of the horse in other countries/Use of the horse as food/Pit ponies/The horse and early man.

This subject is so large therefore that it would be suitable for either a Grade 6 topic; a series of class topics (each based on only one of the group headings given above); a series of individual topics by one child (this presupposes the child is extremely interested in horses); or one class topic provided that each aspect of the subject was not investigated too deeply.

Part Three | Chapter Fifteen

Organizing Topic Groups

Preparation by the teacher

If a topic is to succeed the number and composition of the working groups is obviously of great importance. A group normally consists of between four and seven children, because over seven the group loses cohesion, and if there are less than four the subject matter is often not adequately investigated.

The question of how much information is available on each subject chosen as a group assignment also affects the size of a group when it is formed.

Introducing a topic subject

Before a class is actually broken down into groups it is necessary to introduce the subject matter of the topic. Provided this is well done the children should have obtained enough knowledge to be able to suggest various aspects of the subject which appear suitable for further detailed study by a group. During this process each child will have formed some inclination as to which aspect of the topic will interest him most.

The blackboard outline

During the introduction stage the teacher should have also compiled on the blackboard, with the children's help, a reasonable outline plan of the scope of the topic. This will quite likely coincide roughly with the one which she made when she was preparing for the topic.

The various group assignments should be clearly numbered, and space left for the initials of the children who will eventually form the group.

Problems of grouping children

In many ways it can be said that each group assignment is auctioned, and there is no doubt the teacher will be required to remain calm, careful and, like a good auctioneer, humorously persuasive.

While not wishing to force any child to undertake a group assignment in which it has no interest, the teacher does wish to see that each group is balanced from the point of view of leadership, academic ability, and sociability.

It is almost certain that some group assignments will appear more attractive to the children than others, and the teacher should try to find out which these are by first asking for a quick show of hands for each assignment. Once in possession of this knowledge the teacher is in a good position to try to increase the popularity of the less attractive assignments as she actually forms the groups.

How to form topic groups

The first step is to ask for the names of the children interested in what appears to be the least attractive assignment first and write their initials on the blackboard under the group assignment concerned.

Often only one or two children will opt for this subject, and neither may be suitable as a group leader. For the moment this is unimportant as the teacher will complete the group later.

This process is successively repeated, until one of the more attractive assignments is oversubscribed with children.

When more children wish to join a group than can be allocated to it, the teacher should point out that the assignment is not big enough to give them all enough work, and ask if any are willing to choose another subject. This may result in one or two children changing their mind. If the assignment is still oversubscribed, the teacher should choose the children who will form a well balanced group.

Repeat this process for the remainder of the group assignments until finally a pool of unallocated children of varying ability is formed.

 Once this pool of varied talent is formed the teacher can ask for volunteers to undertake what appears to be the less attractive assignments. Sometimes the teacher can make a direct request to an obvious group leader left in the pool to help out with a particular subject.

The teacher should not suggest that a child should be the leader of the group, for this is something each group must decide for itself.

Having, as it were, auctioned the assignments for a second time, the teacher should assign the few children left in the pool to an appropriate group for the majority of the children will now be eager to start work.

Initially this system may seem a little complicated but among lower juniors it is well worth the time spent in carrying it out, as it results in only a small minority of children working at assignments which they have not actually volunteered for themselves.

As the teacher and children gain experience in forming groups it will be found that the pool of children left after the first auction of assignments is very small, and that the whole process takes but a few minutes.

The internal organization of a topic group

General comment

Having been allocated its working area, each group must learn to organize itself before carrying out a detailed study of a subject. As this initial organization and subsequent working pattern will be required many times, the teacher will be wise if she persuades the children to work to a fixed system. By doing so the very minimum of confusion and argument will take place as the different groups are formed and proceed to work at a series of topics over a number of years.

Such a system also forms a stable working pattern which can be adopted when the children carry out individual topics for themselves.

A group working pattern

A group leader should be elected by mutual consent. If any voting does take place it should be by show of hands. After a group discussion on possible sub-headings for the group assignment, each child should tentatively accept the responsibility for research into one of them.

The group now collects, or is given, information. Every child should have at least three or four books available for this task.

After reading the relevant chapters each child makes a note of the book title and page numbers where the information required can be found. Each child should also make short notes of the type of information available and make a note of any good illustrations.

When a group has located its sources of information it may have to alter its ideas for some of the assignment sub-headings. This problem is discussed, and if necessary, a swift reallocation of work made. At the same time each child receives useful data from the other children in the group, including book titles and page numbers.

Having located their sources of knowledge the children must now be taught to read right through the chapter or pages concerned, close the book and then write up their notes from memory. Spellings, names, dates etc., can be checked later. This drill is repeated by each child for each library book or textbook available.

At this point a child can either discuss his notes and ideas with the teacher, or group leader, or write up a rough account of his findings using the notes he has made. The teacher can then correct this rough draft and suggest other facets of the subject, or further sources of information.

The final copy can then be written up and stored away by the group leader until the topic is correlated at the end.

As each child finishes his own account he can start to produce any illustrations the written work requires.

The group folders which resulted from the topic carried out by a student on teaching practice described in Chapter 10.

This model was produced as part of a topic on the Civil War and was subsequently used as the starting point for the English language topic described in Chapter 9.

Part Three | Chapter Sixteen

The Display and Presentation of Topics

The method of presenting the completed topic so that its contents are appreciated by the whole class, has considerable influence on the organization of the topic while it is in progress. Thus the children must have a clear outline of what the end product of the topic will look like before the work commences. The quickest method of achieving this is to show the class a similar topic of the same grade which has been completed by other children previously.

Sometimes it is not possible to do this, and when faced with the problem of presentation there are many teachers who are in the unfortunate position of having very little artistic ability upon which they can rely to ensure that the children's work is displayed to advantage. Such teachers need help, and in order that they can obtain a certain amount of guidance this chapter has been written. The suggestions given are simple and uncomplicated, for it is realized that it would be useless to describe the wonderful and elaborate techniques employed by those teachers who are lucky enough to be naturally gifted with the art of showmanship.

No method of presenting the children's completed work appears more advantageous than any other, and all can be used with any grade of topic work provided the subject matter concerned is suitable. While this is so, teachers may like to start their own discoveries in topic work by using the grade suggested at the end of each of the following methods of presentation.

Good teachers always try to develop new methods of presentation by adapting those they see used in the world of commerce, for it is intended that the following should only act as stepping-stones for the inexperienced.

In the primary school the end product of a topic usually takes one of these forms:

a An individual or group folder.
b A large scrapbook with the children's work pasted inside.
c A wall mural.
d A tape recording.
e A mime made up about a subject which has been studied.
f A play written and produced by the children.
g A moving film, or filmstrip.
h A model accompanied by explanatory booklets.
i A lesson or lecture given by the children.

Booklets and folders

Quite obviously many sizes of booklets and folders can be used for all grades of topic work and it is pointless to describe each and every possible one. The size and shape of a topic folder will depend mainly on the size of writing paper and the size of any illustrations it may contain.

The construction of the outside cover and the method of attaching the internal pages is however well worth considering. All booklets and folders should be of simple construction as the children will always be in a hurry to show off their completed topic to others. They should also be made sturdy enough to stand up to classroom use for a few weeks, or months, as the case may be. As the size and construction of individual topic books has been discussed in Chapter Eight only class topics are referred to here.

Booklets

1 Where the quantity of information about a subject is small but important, there is usually a good case for duplicating its contents—for example, a pamphlet prepared by a class prior to a visit to a place of interest outside school. A teacher can quite easily type out and produce a duplicated pamphlet of eight pages provided she has a typewriter which is wide enough to hold foolscap paper sideways.

 First, all the children's work should be typed out. Next a

simple booklet should be made by stapling two sheets of foolscap paper together in the middle and folding them along the line of the staples e.g.

Once this is completed the typed work should be cut up, so that each child's work is separate. It can now be arranged and pasted into the small booklet. If there is insufficient space a précis should be made of some of the work or some should, with the child's consent, be left out. Alternatively, any space left over can be used for illustrations or larger headings. Once the complete pamphlet has been mocked-up, it can be retyped for duplicating, and the final booklets constructed with the help of the class.

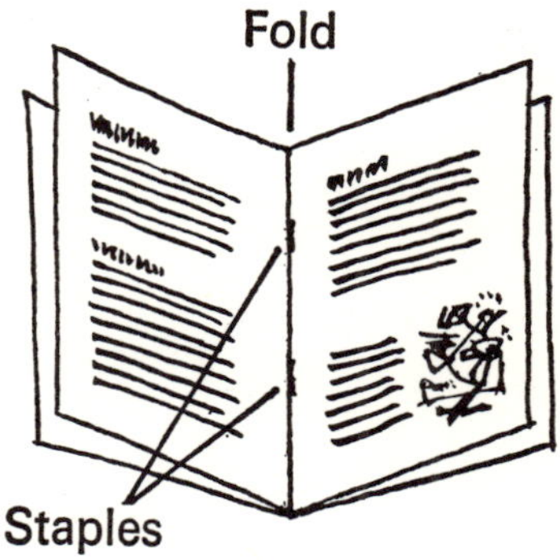

This type of pamphlet is most useful for producing a class magazine.
Size of pamphlet: 8 by 6½ ins.
Useful for: Pamphlet mentioned in Grade 1.
Materials: Foolscap duplicating paper. If less than one hundred copies required a spirit duplicator is ideal.
Long-arm type of stapling machine.

2 Where the teacher wishes the children's actual work to be displayed in individual booklets, the children should complete their work on loose pieces of paper of equal size. Once all the writing and illustrations have been completed an outside cover can be made by using a larger and stiffer piece of paper (cartridge paper) so that the individual sheets can be protected inside it.

Provided a one-inch margin has been left down one side of each page the completed folder can be held together by means of one or two staples fixed right through the entire booklet.

This method is quite

suitable for folders up to about twenty sheets of paper. Suitable size for booklet: 8 by 6 ins (outside).
Suitable for: End product of Topics Grade 4.
Materials: Cartridge or manilla paper, any stapling machine.
3 Once a booklet contains over twenty sheets of paper it is advisable to use paper with file cover holes already punched in it. With this type of paper an outside cover for the booklets can be made by using any manufactured type of file cover containing metal holders inside. Although they are most useful over a period of time, these commercial folder covers can become rather a costly item. Alternatively a simple outside cover can be used by folding some manilla paper and holding the entire booklet together with treasury tags.

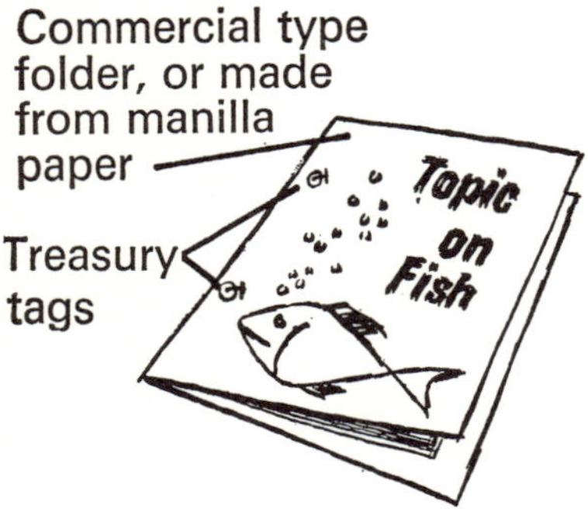

Suitable size for booklet: outside 12 by 9 ins, inside $10\frac{1}{2}$ by 8 ins.
Useful for: End product of any group work in Grades 3 and 4.
Materials: Strong two-hole punch, treasury tags, quarto-size paper, plain and lined, $\frac{1}{3}$-in spacing. Any suitable commercial folder, or manila paper.

Large folders and scrap books

When a class decides to present its topic material by writing and drawing on only one side of their paper before pasting it into a large folder the construction of a simple outside cover becomes quite important. Children find folders and scrap-books bigger than 24 by 18 ins rather awkward to handle in the classroom, and no topic book should be made so heavy that it cannot be easily carried by one child. If this is likely to happen the subject matter should be divided up to produce two or more separate volumes. If the entire folder is thin enough to be held together by staples as illustrated above, then these can be used to bind it together.

Where the cover and contents of the folder are too thick for this process a combination of methods 2 and 3 can be used to make a cover. First, two sheets of cardboard slightly larger than the internal sheets of the folder must be pasted on to a sheet of strong paper capable of taking them side by side while leaving a $1\frac{1}{2}$-in gap between them, and a $1\frac{1}{2}$-in overlap all round.

Next two or three 4-in wide strips of strong paper should be pasted lengthwise down the $1\frac{1}{2}$-in central gap to form a stiff spine for the folder, which is capable of bending.

Once this is completed the overlapping paper from the large outside piece of paper should be pasted down inside, and another large sheet of paper, the exact size of the folder cover, pasted on to complete the inside of the cover. When it has dried out the cover can be folded down the middle to complete it.

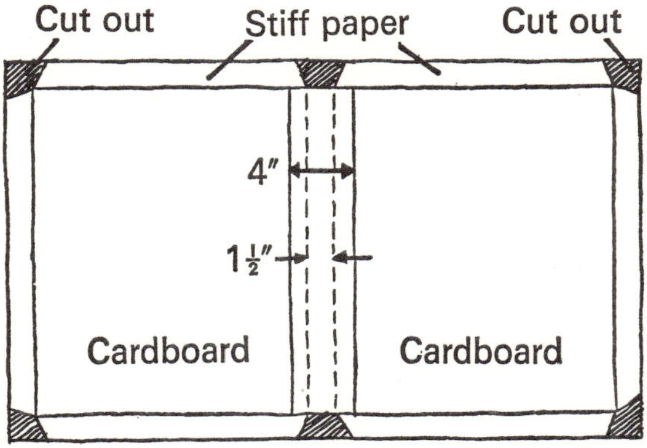

As the separate inside pages of the folder are completed they can be sorted into their correct sequence and stapled together down the left-hand side in batches of ten. When all the sheets are stapled into tens and correctly placed in the folder, two or three holes can be made through the entire folder with a strong leather punch, and long treasury tags can be inserted to hold the entire folder together.

Suitable size: 24 by 18 ins.

Useful for: Grade 3 and topics described in Chapter Three.

Displays and murals

The main problem with this method of displaying a topic is often the difficulty of finding enough wall space on which to place the completed work. Thus before the class decides to make such a display the teacher must assess exactly where and how it can be placed.

Basically there are two types of wall mural, one consisting of a long piece of paper, say 18 ins wide, stretching many feet, upon which the children can paste their work in a suitable sequence so that the entire subject they have been studying can be taken in at a glance.

Suitable size: 18 ins by 12 yds.

Useful for: Grades 1 and 2.

Materials: Frieze paper, assorted colours.

Secondly, a subject can be divided up into sections so that each section can be displayed on a large sheet of paper, say 18 by 20 ins. These individual sheets can then be displayed in various places so that they bring out any sequence there may be in the subject.

Suitable size: 18 by 20 ins.

Useful for: Grades 1 and 2.

Materials: Kitchen paper, various colours.

Of these two methods the second will be more suitable for most classrooms, although the former is most effective, especially if a coloured backing paper is used and the entire mural displayed in a large room such as a school hall.

Wall folder

A wall folder is a combination of a folder and a wall display, and is a simple yet effective way of displaying a topic.

The children's work is pasted on to only one side of large sheets of paper so that a margin of about 4 ins is left at the top of each sheet. The sheets are then placed in order and securely stapled together at the top in batches of ten. Once all the sheets are in order, two pieces of plywood approximately $2\frac{1}{2}$ ins wide by $\frac{1}{2}$ in are required. This wood should be about 3 ins longer than the width of the sheets of paper being used. First one piece of wood should be placed at the back of the sheets at the top and the other on the front of the sheets at the top. When this has been done two screws should be screwed through the top piece of plywood, through the sheets of paper and into the bottom piece of wood, thus holding all the sheets tightly together at the top.

The overlapping timber at the ends can now be used for attaching a piece of string in order that the entire display can be hung on the classroom wall.

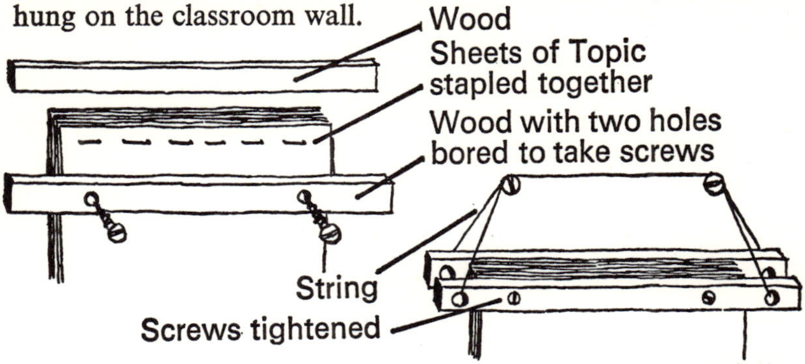

Where the teacher is unable to use a screwdriver successfully, a hammer and nails can be used in place of screws.

The main advantage of this method of display is that a considerable number of topics can be displayed in the classroom at any one time. Two disadvantages are that the children cannot see the entire topic at a glance, and that the individual pages get torn through constantly being lifted up.

Tape recordings

This is an excellent method of presenting a topic, especially if the children's speech requires improvement. The following points are applicable to taped topics in general.

a The overall period of the recording is best kept to less than 45 minutes.

b Direct speech is more effective than indirect speech.

c Sound effects can be used to illustrate a particular point. No sound effect should continue for long periods of time.

d Music is very useful to show the passing of time, particularly if it is faded out and in again.

e Scripts must be well written and parts rehearsed before a recording is taken.

f It is easier to tape the final recording in parts, and not attempt to record the entire production in one session.

g Tapes must be stored and listed carefully so that they are readily available as examples for future work.

Useful for: English topic. See Chapter Nine and Appendix Four.

A lecture or lesson by children

Once they are masters of their subject children love to talk about it, and this should be encouraged in the classroom whenever possible.

This type of end product to a topic is more useful and instructive to all concerned if it takes place regularly and the following suggestions illustrate this point.

1 From Grade 5 onwards children will be completing their own individual topic books. As these subjects are of their own choosing a completed topic can become the basis of a lecture by the child.
2 If one fixed period of time a week is deliberately allocated by the teacher to this work there is soon furious competition by the children for its use.
3 Sometimes it is possible for a group of children to give a lesson on a particular subject. The various parts of a film-strip, a model, or a wall mural can provide the basis for a series of short lectures by various children so that a complete subject is adequately covered.

Suitable for: All Grades except 1.

Mime and plays

Primary children usually require a considerable amount of help from their teacher to produce a successful play or mime. Despite this, the end product of a topic can take these forms and the following points of general interest should be noted.

Plays

1 The central theme of a play must be kept simple, so that the audience sees it clearly.
2 Any research carried out by the children prior to the production of their play can only influence the background to the play as its contents will mostly be fictitious.
3 The use of historical and biblical characters and events should be encouraged as this requires a certain amount of

reading on the part of the children before the writing of the play begins.

4 The use of simple costumes adds to the pleasure given to the audience and the enthusiasm of the actors.

5 If a play is to be the sole end product of a topic, teachers must be sure they are clear about what they intend to teach through the topic before the play starts. If they do not do this the children's delight in play-acting may obscure the true aim of the topic.

Mime

1 Most of the general points concerning plays are applicable to mimes.

2 To follow a mime requires concentration and a certain knowledge of the art of miming, so it is suggested that this method of presenting a topic will only be suitable for classes who already have experience of miming.

3 A mime must have a simple and obvious theme, and it is suggested that to prevent boring the audience it does not last more than twenty minutes.

4 Mimes are extremely good material for recording on moving film.

Suitable for: Topics of all grades.

Moving films and filmstrips

Both films and filmstrips are excellent methods of recording the final results of a topic, but both presuppose that the teacher has considerable photographic ability. Where a topic's end product is naturally photogenic–for example, a play or a wall mural–it may well be worth obtaining help from outside school. Some parents would be delighted to take a moving film of a school play.

Filmstrips of wall murals can be obtained by employing Scholastic Souvenir Co Ltd of Blackpool, who run a nationwide service and produce filmstrips with sub-headings to the teacher's requirements at very low cost.

Teachers should remember that where the final filmstrip is to be in black and white, all illustrations to be photographed should be in black and white, as some colours do not reproduce very well in this medium.

Suitable for: Topics of all grades.

Models

The amount of effort put into making a model for a topic must be kept within reasonable bounds, and the following points observed:

1 A model should only be made when it would be very difficult to illustrate or explain the subject matter in any other way.
2 Whenever a model is made it should always be preceded by a certain amount of research and written work. This aspect of the work should be completed and explanatory booklets produced before the model is started.
3 No model is of any use unless its parts, and their functions, are adequately labelled.
4 In a primary school it is too difficult and quite unnecessary for models to be made to scale unless the main object of the topic is the mathematical aspect of this type of work.
5 A simple model quickly made by the children is far more effective than a complicated model constructed by the teacher over a long period of time with the children's help.

Needlework

Opportunities will occasionally arise for the inclusion of simple forms of needlework in an end product. Such uses might be felt pictures, maps or illustrations sewn and glued together, simple costumes for mimes or playlets. Making period costumes for models, dolls or puppets in connection with a history topic or national costumes for geography topics are probably the most common applications. Cloth covers could also be made for topic folders and booklets.

These two photographs show the covers and some inside pages of a number of individual topic books.

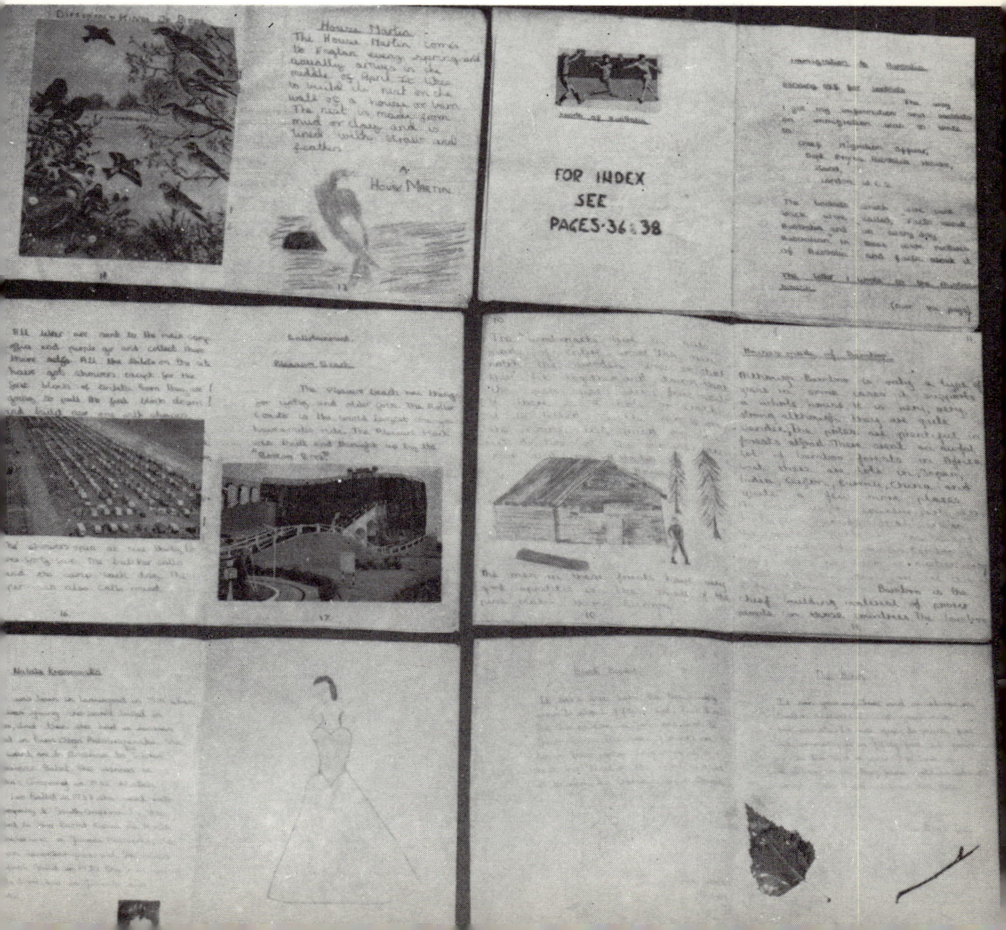

A scene from a nativity play which was the end product of a topic on Christmas.

Part Three | Chapter Seventeen

Making an Appreciation

Any problem is solved more quickly if it is approached in a logical manner and this is what is meant by making an appreciation of a topic. It is essential for the teacher, before a topic is undertaken, to have a clear picture of the aim of the topic, and the method or methods to be adopted. Any doubt or confusion in her mind will soon be communicated to the children and will dissipate the efforts of all.

The problem of approaching a topic can be considered under four headings: aim, factors involved, alternative courses open, final plan.

Naturally the teacher will be guided by the school's scheme of work when seeking her 'aim' for a topic. It is possible to have more than one aim; in which case one must be selected as the 'primary aim'; the remainder then become 'subsidiary aims'. The fewer the aims the easier it is to organize a topic.

If we assume that the teacher in the lowest junior class (7+ to 8+ years) wishes to start topic work and intends to use the Fire Service as her subject, then she might write out her appreciation as follows:

Aim

To visit a place outside school which will arouse intense interest among the children.

The object of this visit is to prepare the children to investigate a subject in such a way that:

1 The class organizes itself so that a different aspect of the subject is studied by each pair of children.
2 New sources of information are introduced such as

brochures of the place visited, advertising material, posters, leaflets and trade journals.

3 The class work is finally displayed in a sequence which shows that all aspects of the subject have been studied.

The teacher may then go on to make the following notes.

Factors involved

1 Most of the class can read quite well.
2 They can write at least half a page of notes per thirty-minute lesson, provided they receive help with spellings and grammar.
3 They know very little about the Fire Service, some have never seen a fire engine except in their picture books.
4 They enjoy painting.
5 The nearest fire station is five miles away.
6 There is no easy bus route to the fire station.
7 Some of the children stay to school meals.
8 Some of the parents will not pay for school visits to places of interest.
9 The least time the whole visit will take is half a day, and the children must be back for school leaving time.
10 As a teacher, I do not know much about the Fire Service myself.

The teacher must now consider ways out of her difficulties and she can do this under the heading 'Alternative Courses Open', but she should only consider practicable courses and put in specific points for and against each one.

Alternative courses open

1 To telephone the fire station and see if they can arrange for a fire engine to visit the school at a fixed time, and for the firemen to explain the engine to the children. Perhaps the headteacher might include a school fire drill to coincide with the firemen's visit. This plan has many advantages but it has the disadvantage that we will not see the fire station, or leave the school grounds.
2 To teach the children from books available and obtainable all about the Fire Service and arrange a visit for myself to

the fire station in order to learn more factual detail, acquire old posters, recruiting leaflets etc. Borrow a moving projector and some training films from the Fire Service, and perhaps persuade a fireman to come into the classroom in his uniform to talk to the children.

The advantages are that this will not disturb the running of the school or require careful timing, but the disadvantages are that it will be less exciting or vivid for the children and picture books are not as good as the real thing.

3 To take the children to the fire station and let them see the firemen at drill on a mock fire, after having spent a few lessons on learning about a fireman's duties in school.

This course will disorganize the school (Miss Blank will have to lose her marking period in order to take 3C). The school fund will have to pay for hire of coach for those parents who will not pay. Will the head say yes? Can I control the children on my own? What happens if a child has an accident? What about food if we are away over lunch time?

Can we visit somewhere else and make a day of it? Are all these problems worth the extra joy and excited interest the children will get from such a visit?

Final plan

Because this is the children's first attempt at a graded topic I feel only course 3 will give them sufficient urge to create the good final product I envisage, therefore I must:

1 Mention to the head that I am thinking of doing a topic on the fire station and get his approval.
2 Telephone the Station Officer at the fire station and see if he will let us visit the station.
3 Visit the fire station and try to arrange some times and dates for the class to visit and at the same time try to obtain any useful literature, films, or new ideas.
4 Explain to the head my outline plan, and agree a time and date for the visit and ask for his help with hire of coach, write to LEA to notify them of intended visit for insurance purposes.

5 See if any other member of the staff wishes to join in hire of coach to visit something near the fire station.
6 Ask head if once details are finalized he will duplicate a letter which every member of my class can take home explaining where, when, why and how we are going on our visit and asking for parents' help with money and a packed lunch if we are going to be out at lunch time.
7 Let canteen staff know at least a week beforehand when the class will not be in for lunch.
8 Start collecting paper, books and other materials for the final topic.
9 Read up a book on fire stations (the National Union of Firemen have produced a very good book on the history and working of the Fire Service).
10 Get head's approval for Mrs Smith, one of the children's mothers I know who is a great help, to join us for the day's visit if she wants to come.
11 Construct a logical, well prepared sequence of ideas for the class to have both before, and after, their visit.
12 Make sure I know exactly what I wish the finished topic to look like bearing in mind that the children may alter it.
13 Finally, check my plan to see that it will accomplish exactly what I stated as my aim in the beginning.

Having taken the trouble to consider carefully the problems of a topic by writing them down on paper, the teacher will be in a very good position to go about her task in the logical and efficient manner which will give her the greatest chance of reaching a successful end product.

Part Three | Chapter Eighteen

Conclusion

Just as a child will slowly progress through the primary school and on to the top of the secondary school, so the main functions of topic work change from one school to the next.

In the infant school a child should learn to be sociable and co-operative, and the teacher must find many opportunities to arouse and satisfy his curiosity. During a child's stay in the junior school he must be given a series of carefully graded topics in order that he can methodically learn through group and individual topics, how to acquire knowledge for himself.

The secondary school should then set out to continue this process by exploiting a child's knowledge of topic work so that it becomes a polished tool readily available as one means of studying any subject.

In many areas of Britain there is a tendency to base much of the work required for the Certificate of Secondary Education upon child centred activities including topics and projects in particular. It is to be hoped that such enlightened ideas will be adopted by all examining bodies for it is time that some educationalists revised their philosophy concerning the purpose of examinations. Basically the only asset of the present type of public examination syllabus is the fact that it forces a child's mind to build up a reasonable system for acquiring fresh knowledge. The subsequent regurgitation of this knowledge at an examination is of very limited importance as the majority of it will have faded from the brain in a remarkably short time. Under our present system of education most of our pupils construct their own method of learning how to learn by a very haphazard system of trial and error. In topic work therefore we should try to place before our pupils a number of situations which encourage them, step by step, to learn how to acquire fresh knowledge systematically, and thereby bring order into what has previously been a hit and miss process.

Obviously to ensure that a child makes ordered progress in this work throughout a school a syllabus for the guidance of the teacher and the child is required. With topic work however the ability to set its contents down on paper during an examination will no longer be regarded as the criterion of success, or failure, as it has been with the type of syllabus tied to an annual examination. With a graded topic syllabus we will only be successful if a child learns when working on his own how to find, organize, and present fresh knowledge methodically, about any subject he wishes to study.

Let us therefore boldly accept the responsibility for equipping the rising generation to think for itself in a way that will give it a chance to cope with the world's problems as they are, and will be in a few years' time. Surely it is becoming quite clear to everyone that we cannot achieve this aim by clinging to the methods of education or mental disciplines we were taught in our youth. Our new schools do not automatically mean better education, they only mean that each teacher has a fresh chance to rethink the problems of educating the children found in his locality, and history shows that too many previous improvements in the administrative structure of education have been nullified by the lack of an energetic effort to try new ideas in the classroom.

To those who have never attempted a child centred activity I say try 'teaching by topics.'

Appendix One

In this appendix are included outline plans for a number of subject topics in each grade.

Grade 1 (See page 45)

Milk

Type of topic: subject/class.
Class: about 28 children.
Time: approximately 8 hours, excluding one afternoon spent at a dairy.
Possible blackboard outline:

1 Cows in a field.
2 Cows going to be milked.
3 The farmer milking cows.
4 The milk churns awaiting collection.
5 The lorry arrives at the farm.
6 The lorry arrives at the central dairy or at the station for loading the churns onto a train.
7 The milk is sterilized in the dairy.
8 The milk is bottled.
9 The milk is crated and loaded on vans.
10 Milk delivered at home and school.
11 Children taking milk to classrooms in the school.
12 Children drinking milk.
13 A nurse weighing and measuring children.
14 Products from milk: cheese, cream, and butter.

The Police

Type of topic: subject/class.

Class: about 40 children.

Time: approximately 8 hours, excluding one afternoon spent at a police station and a two-hour visit to the school by a police car.

Possible blackboard outline:

1 A man sees a pile of papers and milk bottles on a house doorstep.
2 The man decides to rob the house.
3 First the robber telephones the house to see if anyone is in.
4 Now the robber knocks at the front door.
5 He goes round to the back door.
6 He forces a back window.
7 The robber finds some jewels.
8 He looks out of the window.
9 He is seen by a neighbour who is watching the house.
10 She immediately dials 999 and tells the police.
11 A police sergeant receives the 999 call.
12 The sergeant directs a police car to the house.
13 The police car arrives at the house.
14 The robber sees the police car and tries to escape over the garden fence.
15 Another police car arrives.
16 The robber is caught.
17 The robber arrives at the police station.
18 He is put in a room and charged with his crime.
19 The robber is taken before the Judge, the neighbour gives evidence.
20 Robber in prison.

Grade 2 (See page 52)

British Railways

Possible blackboard outline:

GROUP 1. *British Railways*

 Location of the regions/Passenger traffic/Types of coaches/

Engines/Cost per mile/Famous stations in London/Types of uniforms used by employees/Signals used/Famous engines/ Crashes and repairs/Engine and coach workshops/The transport of goods/Train and car ferries.

GROUP 2. *London's Underground*
History of its development/How the tunnels are built/Types of coach and engine used on various lines/Location of the various lines/Types of station, above and below ground/Escalators and lifts used/Cost of travel/Signal and control systems/Various types of employee/History of its use as air raid shelters in Second World War.

GROUP 3. *Our Local Station*
Why it is built where it is/Life of the station master/Type of trains which stop at the station/Cost of travel to nearest big town, the seaside, Europe, airport/Timetable of trains/Signal box.

GROUP 4. *The Life of an Engine Driver*
Where he lives/How much he earns/Where he takes his engine/ His duties while he is driving/Problems of fog, breakdown, snow, etc./Hours he works.

GROUP 5. *Famous Railway Builders*
Richard Trevithick, George Stephenson, Robert Stephenson, Isambard Brunel.

GROUP 5. *Famous Engines*
Trevithick's *Catch Me Who Can*/Blenkinsop's engines/Hedley's *Puffing Billy*/Stephenson's *Rocket*, and *North Star*/Stroudley's engines/Stanier's *Royal Scot* 1927.

GROUP 6. *Private Railways*
The Bluebell Line/Ffestiniog Railway/Tal-y-llyn Railway/ GPO Railway London.

Our Gardens

Possible blackboard outline:

GROUP 1. *Flowers*
Best types for the soil/Annuals, biennials, perennials/My

favourite flower/How to sow and grow flowers/Bulbs and corms.

GROUP 2. *Vegetables*
Grown above ground, and underground/When to plant/How to cut or dig the vegetables/How to bottle, or deep freeze vegetables/How to prepare the soil for various vegetables.

GROUP 3. *Trees and Bushes*
Use of various types, e.g. fruit, flowering, timber producing, screening/How to plant/How to prune/How to transplant/How to store fruit/How to prevent diseases/Roses and their care.

GROUP 4. *Animals in the Garden*
Useful and harmful animals/Animals found in the air, on the ground, underground/Wild animals and domestic animals.

GROUP 5. *Buildings, Machines, and Soil*
Use and building of greenhouses and sheds/Summer house and garages/Manual machines: spades, forks, rakes, watering cans, shears, cutters, lawn mowers/Powered machines: lawn mowers, rotivators, hedge trimmers, saws, water sprays/Furniture: deck chairs, bird tables, swings, slides/Swimming pools: types, heating, maintenance, equipment used in them.

GROUP 6. *Games and Shows*
Garden games played: tennis, clock golf, hide and seek, badminton, swimming, sandpits, snowmen and snowball fights/Shows: showing the produce of the garden, local shows, fêtes, public viewing of private gardens to large houses.

Grade 3 (See page 60)

Astronomy

Possible blackboard outline:

GROUP 1. *The Stars*
Distance from earth and from each other/Meaning of light-years/Types of stars/Nebulae, double stars/Recognizing stars/Various patterns made by the constellations/Observing stars: by optical telescope, radio telescope, spectroscopes/Navigation

by the stars: how done today, how done by Magellan, Drake, Columbus.

GROUP 2. *The Sun and Planets*
The sun: why it is a star/Reasons for sunspots/The solar system/Eclipses of sun, earth, moon/The earth/Its size, weight, shape/What the earth is made from/Why the inclination of the earth gives the four seasons/How we get various lengths of day and night/What we know about Venus, Mercury, Saturn, Jupiter, Uranus, Pluto.

GROUP 3. *Exploring Space*
What is space/Interstellar gas/Comets and their paths/Dangers of space travel/Meteorites/Cosmic and gamma rays/Spaceships and how they are powered, steered, launched, returned to earth/Uses of space/Satellites, sputniks/Their use for exploration of planets, moon, television, weather forecasting, spying.

GROUP 4. *Stars in the Bible, Myth and Legend*
Who named the stars and constellations/The Greek map of the night sky/Old stories of Orion, Hercules, Pegasus/Myths of other lands/Hiawatha, Australian bushmen's stories of stars/The three wise men at Jesus' birth.

GROUP 5. *Astronomy throughout History*
The Babylonians/Ancient Egyptians/Stonehenge/How and why they built objects and buildings with which to study the stars and their calendars/The Incas and Mayas/Counting systems and calendars by the use of the sun, moon, and Venus/History of the earth and its shape as told by the Bible, the Greeks, Copernicus, Galileo.

GROUP 6. *Astrology, Past and Present*
The signs of the zodiac/Their history and use/Telling the future from the stars/Women's magazines/Joseph and Pharoah's dream/The soothsayers of history/Old Moore's Almanack.

Grade 4 (See page 67)

London

Possible blackboard outline:

GROUP 1. *The Government*
The Queen and her duties/Functions of the Houses of Parliament/Details of buildings and Government Offices in Whitehall, e.g. 10 Downing Street.

GROUP 2. *The Docks and River Thames*
Their location/Details of the Port of London Authority/Types of ships using the port/Types of dock and the work of the dockers/Routes of water buses/Places on the river bank such as power stations and the Cutty Sark.

GROUP 3. *The Transport System*
Main line stations/Underground system/Bus routes/Important roads, e.g. Hammersmith Flyover/London's taxis/London Airport.

GROUP 4. *Museums and Historic Buildings*
South Kensington Museums/The British Museum/Clapham Transport Museum/The Tower of London/St Paul's/Westminster Abbey/Guildhall.

GROUP 5. *London's Markets*
The Royal Exchange/Billingsgate/Smithfield/Covent Garden/Petticoat Lane/Hatton Garden.

GROUP 6. *People*
Unusual people: Chelsea Pensioners, Warders at the Tower, Stock Exchange runners, Hon Artillery Co/Useful people: telephone engineers, police, firemen, taxi drivers, sewer workers, hospital staffs, keepers of the Royal Parks, Queen's Messengers.

GROUP 7. *London's Parks*
Battersea Park (Funfair)/Hyde Park (Speakers' Corner)/Kensington Park (Round Pond and Peter Pan)/Green Park (sheep)/St James's Park (birds)/Regents Park (the Zoo).
This outline can be adapted to suit most large towns.

Britain 1700 to 1857

Possible blackboard outline:

GROUP 1. *Inventors and Discoveries*
Hargreaves' Spinning Jenny/Cromptons' Mule/Macadam's roads/Watt's steam engines.

GROUP 2. *Farming Improvements*
The enclosure of land/Townsend's turnips/Coke's sheep/ Blakewell's animal breeding/Tull's farm machinery.

GROUP 3. *Changes in the Home*
Architectural changes in town and country houses/Work of Nash, Robert Adam, William Kent/Changes in landscape gardening by Capability Brown/Changes in furniture by Chippendale, Hepplewhite.

GROUP 4. *Changes in Dress*
The changing styles of the period/The effect of new materials/ Beau Brummell, George III, and Prince Albert/Children's clothes throughout the period.

GROUP 5. *Reformers*
The work of John and Charles Wesley/John Howard/Elizabeth Fry / Lord Shaftesbury / William Wilberforce / Robert Peel / Charles Dickens.

GROUP 6. *The Police Force*
The Town Watch/Henry Fielding's Bow Street Runners/Sir Robert Peel's Metropolitan Police Force—'Bobbies'.

GROUP 7. *Development of Warfare*
War with France, 1756–63/The Navy: ships, press gangs, service, pay and discipline, the 'cat', Lord Nelson/The Duke of Wellington/Waterloo and Trafalgar/The Crimean War, 1853–1856/The Indian Mutiny, 1857.

GROUP 8. *Improvement in Transport*
Trevithick's engine/Stephenson's railways/Telford's roads/ Macadam's road improvements/The Royal Mail coaches, 1785/ Coaching inns/Buses and bicycles/Brindley's canals/Steam ships.

Grade 6 (See page 78)

Coal

Possible blackboard outline:

GROUP 1. *Scottish coalfield*

GROUP 2. *Welsh coalfield*

GROUP 3. *Midlands coalfield*

GROUP 4. *Durham coalfield*

GROUP 5. *Kent coalfield*

Each group is to study the following aspects of coal as it applies to their particular coalfield: History—industrial, pit disasters, etc./Geological—how formed, etc./Geographical—location, sites of mines, towns, industries, railways, ports, structure of coalfield, method of mining employed, spoil heaps/By-products—how made, where made/Types of coal mined, uses to which the various types are put, the requirements of various industries, how supplied/Equipment used for mining coal, carrying it underground/Dangers of coal mining—flooding, dust, explosion, falls of rock and coal, gas, how these are prevented, rescue/Cross section of a coalmine showing how coal is cut and ventilation maintained/Routes for export, and home marketing of coal, use of ships, canals and trains/The life of a miner, his home, pay, holidays, sports.

Explorers

GROUP 1. *Marco Polo*
GROUP 2. *Columbus*
GROUP 3. *Livingstone*
GROUP 4. *Scott*
GROUP 5. *Hilary* (*Sir Edmund*)

Each group is to study the following aspects of their explorers life, and discoveries: Early life, family background/First journey of exploration/First well known journey of discovery/Type of equipment used/Areas discovered and what they contained/Details of any books, maps, poems, written or made by the explorer/When, where, how he died/Animals encountered during journeys/tribes and people met during journeys/Details of the type of weather encountered during journeys/Men who accompanied the explorer/Food eaten during the explorer's journeys/One exciting adventure that befell the explorer.

Another topic, on Horses, similar to this one is given on page 130.

Outlines of individual topics (See page 83)

These outline plans are taken from individual topics actually completed by children in a small village school. Each topic was written in a normal school exercise book containing twenty double-sided pages of lined paper.

Subject—Our School

Pages	Contents
1 to 9	Description of the trees in the school grounds. This included details of the yearly cycle of oak, ash, poplar, birch, apple, pear, elder and holly trees.
10 to 14	An account of the various types of rose trees, their names, colour, size, flowering times, stating if they were standard, bush or rambler.
15 to 19	Details of all the wild flowers found in the school grounds during the summer term.
20	List of classes, names and ages of children and names of teachers.
21	Description of the school cats, and top juniors' fish.
22 to 23	Complete details of the school heating system.
24	Details of school kitchen equipment, staff and meals, provided.
25	Information on the use of the dining hall, hours, capacity, use by classes.
26	Description of staff room and its uses.
27 to 30	A complete description of every type of game the children play in the playground, and their rules.
31 to 34	Drawings of various parts of the school buildings.
35 to 36	Details of various school equipment for PE, radio, tape recorder, music.

37 The school's swimming arrangements and trophies won.

38 Scale plan of the school grounds and buildings.

39 to 40 A complete Index of Contents.

Subject—By the Seashore

Pages	Contents
1 to 3	General description of the seashore visited by the child when on holiday.
4 to 20	Life found in the sea. About a page was devoted to each of the following:

Starfish	Whelks
Jellyfish	Shrimps
Shark	Prawns
Eel	Crab
Seals	Sea Anemone
Dogfish egg	Lobster

21 to 34 Things found on the shore:

Seaweed	Rocks
Breakwaters	Things the sea smooths like pebbles
The beach	
Cliffs	Damage done by storms

35 to 40 Things washed up by the sea:

Shells	Chalk
Limpets	Driftwood
Razor shells	Cans and bottles
Mussels	Sea coal

This topic contained many vivid descriptions of discoveries the child had made on the seashore during her summer holiday along with photographs and postcards of the area concerned.

Subject—Other People's Homes

Pages	Contents
2 to 4	Houses of grass in Africa.
5 to 6	The tents of the Sahara desert.
7 to 8	The Eskimo's igloo.
9 to 12	Houses of wood in Canada, Sweden and Russia.

12 to 14	Houses of Bamboo in Japan and Africa.
15 to 16	The Long Houses of the Dayaks of Borneo.
17 to 18	Building with artificial stone, and cement making in the Medway valley.
19	Houses of cement and flint stone.
20 to 22	Building with iron and steel. The skyscrapers of New York.
23 to 26	Drawings of various types of houses, i.e. tents, huts, cabins, brick houses, semi-detached houses, flats.
27	Details of various types of bricks.
28 to 29	Methods of laying bricks and examples of the various kinds of bonds used by bricklayers, i.e. Flemish, English etc.
30 to 34	Description of brickwork used in the school, home, post office, shop, church.
35 to 36	Wax rubbings of the surfaces of various types of brick. (Similar to bark rubbings.)
37 to 40	A collection of poems about homes, including: 'The Lighthouse' by Marjorie Wilson. 'The Windmill' by E. V. Lucas. 'The Pedlar's Caravan' by W. B. Rands.

Appendix Two

This appendix contains a sample questionnaire as described on page 42, a topic quiz (page 66) and a sample of the type of booklet which could be prepared for an out-of-school visit (page 47).

Sample Questionnaire

For children 7+ to 8+ years.

This questionnaire was drawn up by a teacher as the result of a sparrow finding its way into the classroom.

THE SPARROW

1 What colour feathers has a sparrow?........
2 What colour was its beak?........
3 Find a small picture of a sparrow and glue it on the back of this paper.
4 How many toes has a sparrow?........
5 About how big is a sparrow?........
6 Where do you see lots of sparrows?........
7 How many ounces do you think a sparrow weighs?........
8 Do all sparrows look the same? If not, why not?....................................
9 Why are they different?..................
10 Do you find sparrows all over Britain?......
11 What foods have you seen sparrows eat?....................................
12 What materials do they use for their nest?..................................

13 What do their eggs look like?...............
14 Count the number of sparrows you see in a day and put the number here........
15 On the drawing below put in as many names of the parts of a sparrow as you can find. Try to find the answers by looking at books about birds.

16 Turn over this page and write down any more facts about sparrows you can find.

Topic Quiz

This quiz was prepared to test the children's knowledge after they had carried out a topic on Tudor Seamen.

1 Name four Tudor seamen. (a)..................
(b).............(c)...........(d)...........

2 Name two seamen who sailed right round the world.
(a)...................(b)..................

3 Find three places on the map named after Tudor seamen.
(a).............(b)...........(c)...........

4 What vegetable did Raleigh introduce into England?.....................

5 (i) Who were Queen Elizabeth's
(a) father?...........(b) mother?..........
(c) brother?..........(d) sister?..........
(ii) How long did Queen Elizabeth reign?
....

6 What did Raleigh call the colony he founded in North America and why did he call it this?..
....
....

7 Who singed the King of Spain's beard?.......
Why was it called this?....................
....

8 Name two famous Elizabethan ships..........
....

9 (i) What did Tudor ships look like?.........
....
....
....

(ii) What did Tudor houses look like?.......
....
....
....

10 What colour was Queen Elizabeth's hair?.....

11 (i) How big was the Spanish Armada compared with the English fleet?................
....
(ii) Why did the English win?...............
....
....
....

12 Name three English sports popular in Tudor times.
(a)..................(b)...................
(c)..................

13 (i) Where were prisoners sent to in Elizabeth's reign?........................
(ii) What famous seaman was imprisoned here?
....

14 (i) Name a house near Potters Bar where Queen Elizabeth lived.....................
(ii) What happened to her there?...........
....
....

TOPIC QUIZ PART II

A The letters of the names which are the answers to these three questions are jumbled up. What is the correct name?

(a) Drake set out to fight the Spanish Armada from here. TOLUMPHY...........

(b) A Spanish town. ZIDCA.............

(c) The Spanish Golden City. LE ADDOOR..........

B Here is a crossword

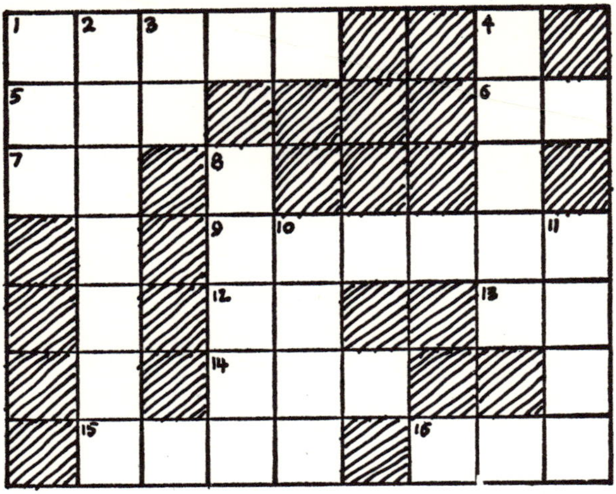

ACROSS

1 He beat the Armada.

5 The Armada — — — away from the British.

6 Dates after Christ's birth are called this.

7 Spanish for 'the'. Remember 'The Golden City'.

9 The Spanish King's name.

12 Two vowels.

13 First two letters of ZOO.

14 Tudor sailors became— — —through not eating proper food.

15 Drake's ship was the 'Golden......'.

16 The British flag ship was the '— — — Royal'.

DOWN

1 First three letters of dream.

2 He put down his cloak for the Queen.

3 Middle two letters of 'sank'.

4 Where the King of Spain's beard was singed.

8 The country owning the Armada.

10 The large space in a ship where the cargo is stored.

11 Sailors ate salt — — — — and ship's biscuit.

The following example is typical of the kind of booklet which should be prepared before an educational visit outside the school is undertaken.

Front cover

Page Two

LONDON TOUR

Approx timetable of our visit

9.00 a.m.	Leave school.
10.00 a.m.	Pass by the Tower of London. We then go past the Bank, St Paul's, the Strand, and the Planetarium
10.30 a.m.	Arrive at Zoo.
2.30 p.m.	Leave Zoo. We then pass by Oxford Street, Marble Arch, Hyde Park Corner, Albert Hall.
3.00 p.m.	Arrive at the Natural History Museum.
4.30 p.m.	Leave Natural History Museum.
5.30 p.m.	Arrive back at school.

Things to remember

Please come in school uniform.
Bring a little money.
Bring a packed lunch and a non-fizzy drink in a plastic bottle.
Bring a note book and pencil.
You may bring your camera if you wish.

If you get lost

Do not wander off very far from where you are lost.
We will look for you.
You can help by:

1 Asking a Policeman, Postman, or Official Attendant to help you.
2 You can dial 999 on any telephone and explain to the POLICE you are lost.

Page Three

LOOK FOR THESE PLACES AS WE TRAVEL BY COACH

Tower of London

This fortress was started by William the Conqueror who built the White Tower on the site of an old Roman fort. During the past 1000 years it has been a royal palace, prison, the Royal Mint, observatory, zoo, and the crown jewels are still kept there.

Tower Bridge

This bridge was built about 100 years ago and is the first bridge as you come up the Thames from the sea.

St Paul's Cathedral

This was designed by Sir Christopher Wren. He began building it just after the Fire of London in 1666 and it was completed in 1710.

Fleet Street

Leaving St Paul's we will travel down Fleet Street where most of our great daily newspapers are published. See how many newspaper buildings you can see and write down their names.

Trafalgar Square

This square was laid out to commemorate the famous sailor Lord Nelson. His statue is on the top of the 184 ft. column that you can see in the middle of the square.

Page Four

QUIZ TIME AT THE ZOO

1 What is a COYPU?
2 What is an APIARY?
3 How do AFRICAN and INDIAN elephants differ?
4 What is an AVIARY?
5 How many mammals are there in the NORTH MAMMAL HOUSE?
6 Write down the names of the two you like best.
7 Why have GIRAFFES long necks?
8 How long is an electric eel?
9 Where do PENGUINS come from?
10 What is an ALLIGATOR?
11 Where do SEA LIONS come from?
12 How many kinds of LIONS are there?
13 How can you spot a TIGER?
14 What are BAIKAL SEALS, and where do they live?
15 Which animal in the children's zoo do you like best?
16 Do RHINOS like water?
17 How many birds with blue feathers can you find?
18 What are their names?
19 Write down the names of four kinds of BEAR.
20 In four lines write down why you would like to revisit the zoo.

Page Five

~MUSEUM QUIZ~

FIND OUT WHAT THESE ARE

B. WHAT IS A COELACANTH?

THE NATURAL HISTORY MUSEUM

This Museum is a branch of the British Museum, dealing with past and present animals and plant life. The crust of the earth is also studied in relation to the fossil remains found in it.
The building was designed by Alfred Waterhouse and opened in the year 1881.

The Dinosaur Gallery shows immense models and actual fossilized skeletons of prehistoric monsters, reptiles and birds. The Whale Room has a model of a Blue Whale 91 feet long.

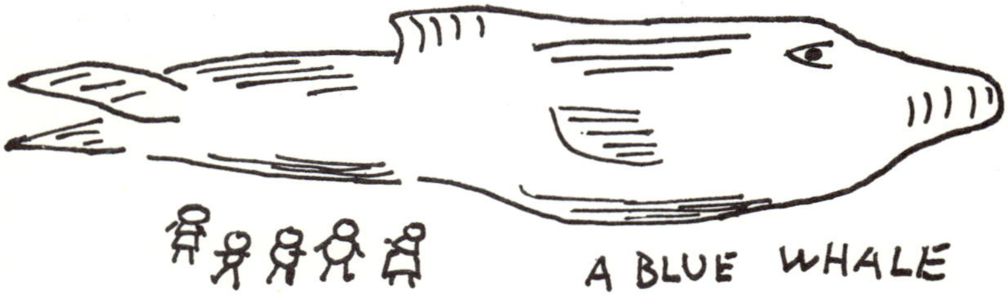

There is a fine collection of elephants in the Main Hall, and a very complete collection of birds' eggs from all over the world. The Museum's research work is well known, and its reference library is one of the finest to be found anywhere.

KEEP BRITAIN TIDY
DO NOT DROP YOUR RUBBISH
TAKE IT HOME

Page Seven

WHAT TO DO WHEN YOU RETURN TO SCHOOL NEXT DAY

1 Complete the quizzes on separate paper. Then hand them in to your teacher.
2 Write any 'Thank you' letters to people who have helped you with your visit
3 Write a short account of about half a page describing that part of the visit you enjoyed most.
4 Paint a picture connected with London, or make a model of something you saw.
5 Make a display of any picture cards, pamphlets, etc, you bought on the tour.

Page Eight

THE WIND'S HOLIDAY

The wind woke up one sunny morn,
He blew and scattered all the corn.

He felt tired, not very gay,
He thought he'd have a holiday.

'Blow off our seeds that they may grow,'
The flowers did say, they did not know.

Oh! no poor flowers you're at your best,
I'm off to have a nice long rest.

So he to London town did go,
To see the sights he didn't know.

The Palace, Big Ben, Hyde Park and the Zoo,
The Abbey, the river, and Marble Arch too.

He, as the wind, had no need of a cabby,
As he swept along past Westminster Abbey.

Soon he got tired of his holiday spree,
So back he went to the quiet country.

And so the flowers waited one whole week,
Until to the wind they dared to speak.

'We hope you've had a lovely rest,
Blow off our seeds. Please do your best.'

And so the wind did as they pleased,
And scattered all their tiny seeds.

David
Aged 11 years

Appendix Three

This contains extracts from the work produced by children on some of the topics mentioned elsewhere in the book.

Fires and fire fighting (Grade 1, page 45)

Class: 30 children aged 6, 7 and retarded 8+ years.

Marion aged 6+ years
The house is on fire and the firemen are coming. You dial 999 to get the firemen.

Kevin aged 6 years
When anyone sees a fire they should dial 999. You tell the operator where it is, or what has crashed, and if you know the name of the road, tell it. Also tell them whether you want fire, police, or ambulance. If it is not an emergency you dial 4444 for fire.

Beverley aged 7+ years
The call comes through to the Control Room and a lady answers it, and makes a note of it. At the same time it goes on a tape recorder. The operator passes on any instructions to the ambulance.

Wendy aged 8+ years
When the alarm goes, the firemen are upstairs and when they hear the alarm they go down the slippery pole and put their hats on downstairs, and get their ladders.

Jane aged 6 years
The last thing that the fireman does before he goes out of the station is to open the doors. Sub-Officer Smith picks up the message then he pulls the rope that hangs down from the ceiling at the side of the fire engine and the doors fold apart, and the engine is on its way.

Angela aged 6 years
On the way to the fire one of the firemen is in contact with the Control Room.

Susan aged 6 years
A fireman runs to the hydrant. Here he will get some water to put on the fire.

Garry aged 8 years
When the fire is over the firemen have to roll the hoses up and put them in the fire engine and go back to the station. When they get back they stand to attention.

Lesley aged 7 years
After the firemen come back to the station they are not allowed to go and eat and drink before they have been dismissed. Then they go and check the fire engine.

Farm animals in Britain (Grade 6, page 78)

Type of groups: individual topics contributing to independent groups.
Class: 36 children aged 11 years.
Time: about 24 hours.

General details

The end product of this topic was five thick booklets (13 by 9 ins) containing about 40 pages of written work by the children. A great deal of correspondence developed between the class and various firms connected with the subject and all this as well as the advertising material obtained was included in the booklets. The exterior of each book was decorated by cutting out the more colourful advertisements and pasting them on the front cover.

As this topic covered such a wide field it is only possible to give one extract from the work of each group.

BRITISH CATTLE GROUP

Brief outline of subjects included in group booklet

Breeds of cows/Milking cows/A milking parlour/Milking apparatus/Marking cows/By-products of cows/Storing meat/ Where cows are found in Britain/The parts of a cow/Sale of cattle / Calves / Bulls / Bullocks / Smithfield market / Correspondence and advertisements.

Extract from work on Milking by Pat aged 11 years 2 months

Milking is done mostly in a cow shed. Another word for a milking shed is a milking parlour. First of all you keep them occupied by feeding them. Then you scrub the cow's hindquarters and then you wash the flank, tail and udder with a clean cloth and water. The cows have to be scrubbed and washed because dirt might go on to the milk, and it will not be fit for drinking. When the milking starts they put small rubber-lined cups over their teats which squeeze them and draw the milk out into a pipe which goes into a churn, or goes into a tank at the end of the milking parlour. This tank is called a cooler. In the cooler running water in the pipes cools the milk, because the milk goes over the pipes and it makes it cool. Then the milk is strained and it goes into the churns. After this you milk the cows by hand to get the last drop of milk out of them. When all the milking is finished you clean all the milking apparatus with clean water.

PIG AND GOAT GROUP

Brief outline of subjects included in group booklet

Breeds of pigs/A sow and her piglets/Pigsties/A plan of a modern pigsty/Pig diseases/Parts of a pig/Where bacon comes from/Pig troughs and bedding/Pig foods/Pigskin and products/ Cuts of pork/History of pig breeding/Sale and export of pigs/ Tinned food from pigs/The poem 'The Poor Man's Pig' by

Edmund Blunden/Goat breeding/Feeding/Keeping/Milking/Sale/Meat/Wild goats.

Extract on Pig Keeping by Joan aged 11 years 0 months
You often find a pig on a smallholding or farm because the pig gives a quicker return of meat. A farmer should start with a few pigs and then get more. One advantage in keeping pigs by a small farmer is that he can get boys or women to do the work as it is not difficult. It is usually better to breed and feed pigs for the following reasons:

a It usually costs less to produce pigs than to buy them.
b Home bred pigs usually fatten more easily.
c There is less risk of having swine fever.
d The pig keeper finds it costs less at the market prices.

HORSES, PONIES AND DONKEYS GROUP

Brief outline of subjects included in group booklet

All these animals were studied under the following headings: Breeds/How to look after them/Feeding/Illnesses/Skeleton structure/Riding equipment/Children's clubs connected with these animals/Poems and stories connected with them, including *Black Beauty* by Anna Sewell/Housing these animals/History of animals and their part in man's development/Cost of animals/Export trade in live and dead animals/Products from animals/Modern uses of horses/Polo/Racing/Show jumping.

Extract from work on Riding by Mary aged 11 years 0 months
Before you start out on a ride you should be careful that the girth is not loose. When leading a horse on the public highway you always lead it on the right-hand side of the road, facing the traffic, and you also keep yourself between the cars and the horse. You should always lead a horse with your left hand. You must never canter a horse on the road because if you go downhill at a canter you can break the horse's two front knees, because its steel shoes may slip on the tarmac.

SHEEP GROUP

Brief outline of subjects included in group booklet

 Breeds of sheep and where they are found/How wool comes

from sheep/How wool is made and the things it is made into/ Handling sheep on a farm/Marketing sheep/Prices of sheep/ How lambs are born/Why farmers like early lambs/How to feed a lamb that has lost its mother/Diseases of sheep/Sheep shows/ Names given to the different ages of sheep/Sheep dipping/ Types of joints from sheep/Names of various parts of sheep/ Development of sheep since 1700.

Extract from work on sheep dipping by June aged 11 years 5 months
These flies lay their eggs in a damp and dirty spot in the sheep's fleece. Out of these eggs hatch little maggots that feed on the living flesh of the sheep. These maggots can eat away the sheep and it can be eaten alive. The maggots may strike the sheep between April and October. It is therefore very troublesome in the summer. To get rid of this they have to put the sheep through a dipper, and afterwards it keeps the maggots away. If the maggots have chosen a part of the sheep's fleece to lay their eggs on it will turn brown.

The Stuart Period (Grade 4, page 67)

Class: 28 children 9+ to 10+ years.

The period was covered by splitting the class up into five groups, each dealing with one important item of the Stuart period. This allowed each group to go into their subject in detail. The following shows what information each group found, and how they organized their Individual Group booklets on these subjects.

1 James I. 2 John Bunyan. 3 The Civil War. 4 The Puritans. 5 Fire of London.

BOOKLET ON JAMES I
Front folder of booklet
Main title: The Stuarts.
Subtitle: James I's reign, 1603–1625.
Illustration: the cover contained five small sketches in coloured crayon—James I, the Bible, Guy Fawkes, a sailor and a farmer. The last two were shown in the normal dress of the period.

Page	*Details*
1	The title page which also contained the names of the children who wrote the booklet.
2	Index of contents.
3	Description of how the work was carried out.
4	Diagram showing the order in which the Stuart kings and their wives took the throne starting with James I.
5	A map of James I's journey from Scotland to London to accept the English throne with written description of that journey.
6	Picture of James I with his family and written description of each member of the family.
7	Details of James I and his connection with the Authorized Version of the Bible.
8	Description of how the work on the new Bible was organized.
9	Further details of the translation of the Bible.
10	Written work concerning the planning of the Gunpowder Plot with drawings of Guy Fawkes.
11	Drawing of all the Gunpowder Plot members and description of what happened to them.
13	Drawings and descriptions of the clothes worn during James I's reign. Price list of clothes of various sorts. How wigs were made.
15	Photographs of dolls dressed by the children in early Stuart costumes.

BOOKLET ON JOHN BUNYAN

Front of folder booklet

Main title: The Stuarts.

Subtitle: John Bunyan.

Illustration: Coloured crayon drawing of John Bunyan standing beside a village cross.

Page	*Details*
1	The title page containing the names and ages of the children who wrote the booklet.
2	Complete index of contents.
3	Head and shoulder linocut of John Bunyan.

4 Description of how the booklet was compiled.

5 The writing on this page is under two headings. One explains how books were printed in Bunyan's time, the other describes the tools used by printers, and what types of press were used.

6 Seven small pencil sketches of the dress of puritan men, women and children.

7/8 A history of John Bunyan's life. Also a picture of Bedford jail where Bunyan was imprisoned.

9/10 Description of Thomas Bunyan (John Bunyan's father) and his life as a tinker. More details of Thomas Bunyan's family follow a water colour of John Bunyan in prison.

11 People's dress in Bunyan's time, pictures, and list of articles and their cost.

13 Four drawings giving details of the printing trade in Stuart times.

14 A list of John Bunyan's writings with a short précis of each.

16 The original and modern versions of 'Who would true valour see', set out side by side for comparison.

BOOKLET ON THE CIVIL WAR

Front of folder booklet

Main title: The Stuarts.

Subtitle: The Civil War.

Illustration: five separate linocuts—one of an oak tree and the dates 1642–1649 underneath, two of oak tree outlines, one head and shoulders outline of Cromwell and one of Charles I.

Page *Details*

1 The title page containing the names of the children who wrote the booklet.

2 Large linocut, 6 by 6 ins, of a Roundhead soldier.

3 Index of contents.

4 Map of England giving details of where the main battles of the war were fought.

5 Written explanation of reasons why Charles I quarrelled with his Parliament.

6 Drawing in colour of a Cavalier on horseback.
7 Map of England showing the ground held by both sides in 1642.
8 Description of the type of life Charles I had as a boy.
9 Description of Oliver Cromwell's early boyhood.
10 Drawing of a Roundhead soldier.
11 Writing and drawings concerned with Prince Rupert's dog 'Boy'.
13 Large drawing of Prince Rupert on horseback.
14 Details of the New Model Army.
16 Carefully drawn illustrations of many of the weapons used during the Civil War.
17 Two large drawings of soldiers in the armour used at the beginning of the Civil War.
18 A picture of a skirmish between Roundheads and Cavaliers.

BOOKLET ON THE FIRE OF LONDON

Front of folder booklet

Main title: The Stuarts.

Subtitle: The Fire of London.

Illustration: Photograph of St Paul's Cathedral taken just after the 1939–45 war showing ruined buildings in the foreground.

Page *Details*

1 Title page containing list of children who wrote the booklet.
2 Half a page on how the children organized and wrote the booklet.
3 Index of contents.
4 Details of the Great Plague that preceeded the Fire of London.
5 Head and shoulders linocut of Samuel Pepys.
6 One page of Samuel Pepys' diary describing the Fire in his own words.
7 Copy of Pepys' shorthand and its meaning in modern English.
8 Photograph of Wren's design of St Paul's which Charles II accepted 1667.

9 Description of the Fire of London compiled by the children from many different sources.

10 How the fire started, and a photograph of Wren's portrait by Kneller painted 1711.

12 Details of Christopher Wren's life including a list of buildings he designed and photographs of many of them.

BOOKLET ON THE PURITANS

Front of folder booklet

Main title: The Stuarts.

Subtitle: The Puritans.

Illustration: A very simple outline drawing of a puritan woman.

Page	*Details*
1	Title page with a list of children who wrote the booklet.
2	Index of contents.
3	Page description of the problems found by the children when making the booklet.
4	An attractive diagram, showing various aspects of puritan life and dress.
5	Details of how the puritans dressed, and drawings of puritan children.
7	Writing on who the puritans were and their beliefs.
9	Drawing of the Mayflower barn at Jordans, Bucks.
10	Details of life in a puritan home.
11	Drawings of furniture used about 1600.
12	A short account of the voyage of the *Mayflower* to America.
14	How the puritans progressed in America, and drawings of *Mayflower* and the puritans landing.

The following poem was part of the end product of a Grade 6 topic on Australia.

IMMIGRATION

On a cold winter's day
In the foggy UK,
My great aunty Dahlia
In sunny Australia,
Sent me from out there
A young Koala bear.

As the bear grew up bigger,
This sweet little 'digger'
Spun wondrous tales
Of Australia's trails,
With their tropical breeze,
And brilliant blue seas.

Without second thought,
I grabbed my passport,
And by fast aeroplane
To Australia I came,
To say 'How-do-you-do'
To each old Kangaroo.

So don't stand and wonder,
Just join us down under,
Via a house on the Strand,
Where you'll soon understand,
How to get information
About your immigration.

Elizabeth, aged 11 years

Appendix Four

This appendix contains outline plans for two topics on English as described in Chapter Nine with some extracts from the work produced.

JOSEPH SHINER

Topic subject: all aspects of English.
Type of group: independent topic group.
Class: 28 children aged 10+ years.
Time: about 20 hours.
Aim: to make a tape recording suitable for broadcasting and thereby improve all aspects of the children's standard of English.

Outline plan of topic

GROUP 1 (seven children) *Joseph Shiner's Early Life*
Where Joseph lived, and how he managed to persuade his parents to let him join the Roundheads.
GROUP 2 (six children) *Joseph Trains to be a Soldier*
How Joseph met Oliver Cromwell and joined the army/How he trained to be a pikeman in General Fairfax's First of Foot.
GROUP 3 (eight children) *Joseph's First Battle*
How the battle started/Joseph kills his first man/Joseph is captured and escapes/How he returned to his Regiment.
GROUP 4 (seven children) *Joseph's Death*
Joseph's final battle/He is wounded and taken from the battle by his friend Abraham/He is nearly caught by Royalists/Abraham takes him to his mother/He dies.

General comment

The number of children in each group was too large for every child to play its full part in the topic. The outline of the topic was not prepared in enough detail by the children and the teacher.

The teacher learnt from these mistakes and the second attempt at an English topic of this type was much more successful. See details on page 187.

Extract from English Topic, Joseph Shiner

This extract is taken from the start of the topic and shows the children's first attempt at an English topic. Notice the lack of clarity in layout and weak script when it is compared with extract given on page 188.

THE LIFE OF JOSEPH SHINER

I was born in an old cottage on the corner of Cole Green. It was a windy day when I was born. I was born on a Thursday at 8.25 p.m. 1624. My father's name was Duncan. Each morning he got up early and went hunting. 'Go and get my gun, Joseph,' he would say.

'No why don't you ask mother' I replied.

My parents were not very rich and not very poor, but we did need a bit more money, so I decided upon ways to get money. Every suggestion I made my parents turned down.

'Couldn't I go and work down at the blacksmith's shop,' I asked.

'No you can't,' replied my mother.

'What about working down at the baker's?' I asked again.

'If you go there and work you will be there from very early in the morning until late at night, and that won't give you any time to get any sleep at all. No, and that's final,' said my mother.

Each morning I have to feed the horses and chickens. 'Go and fetch me some corn please Dad,' I said.

'No it's your job not mine,' answered Dad.

One morning I heard my parents discussing an important matter. They were talking something about a war.

'Supposing they want me to fight in a battle. How will you look after the children?' my father asked my mother.

'I don't know, but let us not think about it my dear,' replied my mother.
Suddenly the idea struck me. Why didn't I join one of the armies? I could take my friend Abraham with me.
'Please let me join the Roundheads,' I pleaded, 'I know Abraham will come with me.'
'Oh, you had better ask your father,' my mother replied.
'Father, will you let me go to war as a Roundhead?' I asked.
My father replied, 'I should think we could let you go with Abraham.'
When it was time to go it was all 'Farewells' and 'Good-byes'. My mother was in tears and she said, 'Good-bye Joseph. Do look after yourself.'

PRISCILLA MULLINS

Topic subject: All Aspects of English.
Type of group: Independent.
Class: 38 children aged 10+ years.
Time: About 16 hours.
Aim: To improve all aspects of the children's use of the English language by making a tape recording. It was decided to make a forty-minute recording concerning the life of a seventeenth-century Quaker girl called Priscilla Mullins.

Outline plan of topic

GROUP 1 (nine children) *Priscilla's Early Life*		
Scene 1	A holiday when Priscilla is 8 years old	3 children
Scene 2	Priscilla's first job in a shop.	3 children
Scene 3	A journey to Plymouth when 18 years old.	3 children
GROUP 2 (ten children) *A Visit to Holland*		
Scene 1	Journey aboard the *Speedwell* to Holland.	4 children
Scene 2	In Holland and return to England.	3 children
Scene 3	Priscilla's arrival in Plymouth.	3 children

GROUP 3 (nine children) *Aboard the 'Mayflower'*		
Scene 1	The storm.	3 children
Scene 2	After the storm a stowaway is found.	3 children
Scene 3	Landing in America.	3 children
GROUP 4 (ten children) *America and Priscilla's Death*		
Scene 1	Building the settlement.	2 children
Scene 2	Part 1 The Plague.	3 children
	Part 2 An adventure in the woods.	3 children
Scene 3	Old age and Priscilla's death.	2 children

Comment

To prevent the topic recording taking more than forty minutes, each scene had to be reduced to one sheet of foolscap. This resulted in a script which only contained bright, fast-moving scenes.

This was the teacher's second attempt at an English topic. Notice the general improvement in both layout and content as compared with the extract of English topic given on page 186.

Extract from English Topic, Priscilla Mullins

This extract is taken from the work of Group 2 Scene 3—Priscilla's arrival at Plymouth.

PRISCILLA MULLINS ARRIVES AT PLYMOUTH

SCENE: As Priscilla's family see the sea they notice the *Mayflower* waiting for passengers.

Mother 'Look children! There is the sea, and the *Mayflower* too. I wonder if father is on board yet.'

Priscilla 'Do you think father can see us from there mother?'

Mother 'He might, but I don't think he will notice us until we are a lot nearer, Priscilla.'

John 'Mummy will Daddy really be on board that big boat?'

Mother 'John darling, how many times have I to tell you it is not a boat, but a ship?'

John 'I always call ships, boats. I like the word boat better than ship.'

 Priscilla 'Oh mother do look at all those people. Are you

sure we won't get lost in that crowd getting on board ship?'

John 'Look Mummy! There's Daddy! Daddy! Daddy! I'm here!'

Priscilla 'Oh yes! I can see him. Can't you Mummy?'

Mother 'Yes dear. Wave, Priscilla.'

SCENE: On board the *Mayflower*. The Mullins family are pushing through the crowd on deck looking for Mr Mullins when the Captain meets them.

Captain Standish 'Good afternoon ladies. I am Captain Standish of this ship and I hope you will enjoy your trip to America.'

Mother 'Good afternoon to you Captain. Perhaps you can tell me where Mr Mullins is?'

Captain 'Yes I think so. He is over there by the main sail.'

Mother 'Thank you very much Captain. Now if you two perishers will stop playing about I will take you to see your father.'

Priscilla 'Daddy! Daddy darling! I have missed you!'

Mr Mullins 'Priscilla. You startled me.'

Mother 'Jack darling. Thank God we have found you again!'

Index